Happy Father's Day

From the Advance

Ohio Farm

Ohio Farm

By Wheeler McMillen

With Illustrations by
John D. Firestone and Associates

Ohio State University Press

Copyright © 1974 by the Ohio State University Press
All Rights Reserved.
Manufactured in the United States of America

Library of Congress Cataloguing in Publication Data
McMillen, Wheeler
Ohio Farm.

1. Farm life—Ohio. I. Title
S521.5.O3M3   917.71   74-12216
ISBN 0-8142-0217-9

Dedication

To Robert Doane McMillen
who has inherited the virtues of
his grandparents and mother without
acquiring his father's faults

Contents

Preface

These pages attempt to describe what went on in field, barn, house, and our rural neighborhood during the period my farmer father chose to call his "golden years"—roughly, from 1900 to 1915. Engine power and science had not yet begun to transform midwestern farming into the more intense kind of business it has since become; nor had they yet altered the countryside social customs.

The men who farmed and the ways they farmed in those years have now faded into history. Their times fell in between the pioneer, largely subsistence farming of the early nineteenth century and the cash economy agriculture that the middle third of the twentieth century has developed. By producing enormous amounts of basic wealth that built industrial America, they made history, too.

If one were to try today to farm on the same scale in the same manner and with the same equipment, he would be hopelessly lost. Yet in those times a good farmer could prosper and become independent. My father did both. This is primarily his story.

The small details of the ever changing seasons, whether at work or at fun, I have tried to report faithfully. In verification I can say, first of all, that I was there. Father's account books and concise diaries have been most helpful. Because this was a family farm, and because as a junior member of the family I participated in nearly all that went on, some personal intrusion into the story has seemed to be unavoidable; for this, my mild apologies are presented.

Farm life in those days across the corn belt to as far as the one-hundredth meridian was much the same as in western Ohio. Most of the details told here, with slight variations, will accord with the experiences of those who farmed then elsewhere in the Midwest.

No one will again undergo the experiences of that period. It has been a pleasure to recall them, and to try to record some of that history in terms of one Ohio farmer, his community, and its people.

Wheeler McMillen

Ohio Farm

L. D. McMillen, 1858–1928

Woodcut engraving by unknown artist

Chapter 1

The Years of Copper

The folkways and farm ways that rural America followed until well into the first quarter of the twentieth century were not as they are now. The ruthless bulldozers of change have shoved them into an almost forgotten past. Within that irrecoverable and unrepeatable period, farm living was rich with fascinating environment and events; richer, perhaps, in retrospect than it seemed to be at the time.

My farmer father referred to a portion of that period, roughly from 1900 to 1915, as his "Golden Years." Though the prime intent of this book is to record the methods and incidents of that decade and a half, it will also be a sort of biography of Father. He deserved one. So, meet him now.

Six feet tall in his socks, lithe and muscular though never thin, he walked and stood erectly. His erectness was no soldierly strut; he would not have known how to strut. Bronzed, blue-eyed, with sandy hair, partly bald, mustache plainly cropped, always neat, modestly dignified, companionable but never effusive, he was a complete man about whom or to whom no one ever spoke without respect.

Over the years it was to become my privilege to meet thousands of farmers from coast to coast. Consciously, often, and many times unconsciously, they have been compared with Dad, and never to his disadvantage. He was representative. That he was average I cannot quite agree—though he would have said that he was—for he was above average, and maybe he was not quite typical. But he represented the independent, fairminded, and intelligent American of his time who was then making a good living at tilling the soil. When the orators spoke of farmers as "the backbone of the nation," they had in mind men such as he.

Here, perhaps, is the place to note that a sort of federal and official confirmation was placed upon Father's designation of his Golden Years. When the agricultural brain-trusters of the Franklin D. Roosevelt administration decided to establish what they called a standard of "parity" for farm prices, they adopted those of 1910–14, the latter part of his chosen period. Through many succeeding Congresses farm price legislation continued to consider those years as the base from which to measure a fair exchange value between farm products and other commodities.

Father did not reach those Golden Years easily; although he enjoyed the road, the going must at times have seemed hard and slow. He was born during the presidency of James Buchanan in the year of the Lincoln-Douglas debates, 1858. The tree-shaded McMillen homestead stood by the banks of the Portage River, four miles east of Bowling Green, in Center Township, Wood County, Ohio. There his childhood and youth were spent. He seldom spoke of his growing-up years, except for occasional references to small adventures at

4

skating and swimming, or to the rough jobs of clearing new land.

No doubt he had as many ancestors as anyone else. If any were famous, no legend of them was ever handed down; if any were infamous, they had been forgotten. Father did occasionally mention his paternal grandfather, Alexander McMillen, who had been born in what is now Pittsburgh and had survived until 1868. An orphan, Alexander had been raised by a friendly family and had learned the cobbler's trade. At seventeen he had joined his two older brothers, and the three floated by raft down the Ohio River to Marietta. There, Alexander disembarked; the other two went on down the river. "We never heard what became of them," Father said. Pioneer families often scattered.

His maternal grandfather, John Carter, was a Wood County pioneer who paid for his acres by hunting wolves. The state offered $4.25 for scalps of grown wolves, and $2.50 for cubs. John must have been a mighty hunter. An old newspaper clipping stated that during 1843 he had collected more than a fourth of all the wolf bounties paid that year in Wood County.

The fabulous person in the family seems to have been Father's mother, Marilla. Of her it was said that she knew all the old herb and folk remedies, and that she was always first to hurry to the bedside of any neighbor in misfortune. She brought up not only her own four sons and one daughter but twenty-two other boys and girls, most of whom were orphans from related families. She was a sort of personal "institution" who offered love and care to any motherless child.

Until Father was past thirty, he and his brothers ran their home farm. Their father had died in 1884 after

5

several years of poor health. The boys had little time to go to school. Although his formal education was measured in a small total of months—parts of a few short terms at the nearby district school—Father read widely and became a well-informed and in many ways a well-educated man. In his later years acquaintances sometimes asked what college he had attended. Books were scarce as he grew up, and so was cash; but in his twenties he bought for seventy-five cents a copy of *The Science of Farming*, and for $2.50 another book called *The American Stock Book*.

He had been named Lewis, to which at some point he chose to add a "D." Relatives and close friends called him "Lew." "L. D. McMillen" was invariably his signature, and many acquaintances called him "L.D."

In Mother's autograph album, on Washington's Birthday, 1885, he wrote, "With best wishes, I remain your friend, L. D. McMillen." How long before that they had been acquainted I do not know, but nearly three years later, in the laconic and reticent diary that he kept for much of his life, a two-word entry appeared for December 28, 1887: "Got married." His bride, a bright-eyed, cheerful little brunette, had been the hired girl in the home of Bowling Green's leading merchant. He was 29, and she was 23. For forty years they were to be congenial partners.

During the spring of that year Father crossed the Mississippi to work for a season with cousins who had settled in northwestern Iowa. He wanted to get started at farming for himself. Wood County's soil, rich and black, already was selling for $60 and even $80 an acre, too much for a young man with very little capital. (It sells for $600 to $1,000 an acre now!) For that Iowa summer he helped to make hay and to tend crops, hunted prairie chickens, and explored the country. Ohio, he decided, suited him better.

His search led fifty miles southward from the old Portage River home, to Hardin County. There, in Marion Township, Section One, he found 125 acres that looked good and could be bought for $35 an acre. It had a log house, a log barn, and a straw-covered shed, few fences or other improvements, and, he was to learn, rather poor drainage.

Early in 1891, just in time for the depression of that decade to begin, Father and Mother and their baby daughter moved into the old house. By wagon team they brought down from Wood County their few furnishings and some essential field implements.

The first cash entries in his account book mentioned butter at twenty cents a pound and chickens that sold at five and a half cents. That fall there came a $33 doctor's bill, $13.83 for a cemetery lot, and $26.95 for "undertaker's bill." The baby girl had died.

The next expenditure, noted a week later, was three dollars, a new hat for Mother. That, I am sure, Father did not count as an extravagance.

Before long, eggs were being sold for as little as nine cents and butter for as little as twelve. Hogs brought four cents a pound and steers $3.30 a hundred pounds. Those were the copper years, when every penny counted.

Prices were not supported. No farmer even dreamed about receiving federal aid. Benjamin Harrison was finishing his presidential term, and Grover Cleveland just five years earlier had vetoed an appropriation to buy seeds for drouth-broken farmers in Texas. While agreeing that the cause was worthy, "It is for the people to support the government," he wrote, "not for the government to support the people."

Whatever the prices, Father and Mother intended to get ahead and they did. They added occasionally to their stock of comforts, and took time off for bits of pleasure. The record notes $1.50 spent at the county fair, $7.00 twice a year for Mother to visit the relatives back in Wood County, and $19.70 for Father's 1893 trip to the Chicago World's Fair. They did not believe in uninterrupted drudgery.

Earlier that year an expenditure of $8.00 was noted; it was the doctor's fee for attending at my birth—probably a fair valuation at the time. On the same date Father also paid out $11.62 for a bushel and a half of red clover seed, and on the first anniversary bought "Doc," a roan buggy horse for $85. Doc proved to be an interesting character; he will be mentioned again.

Before the end of 1895, although depression prices still prevailed, the $2,000 mortgage was paid off. Plans were made to replace the little old log barn. The folks wanted a new house, too, but any prudent farmer knew that a good barn would help to pay for a house but that a house could not pay for a barn.

The log house was genuine enough, though not the kind of log cabin in which Ohio presidents had been born. The original builder had had bigger ideas. He had constructed a two-story house, two rooms below and two above, with an interior staircase. A later occupant had framed two more rooms at the rear, and had enclosed the whole in planed, overlapped horizontal siding. To the casual eye the house looked like any other

8

modest frame structure, though the thick window frames and doorways of the front part betrayed the log walls concealed within.

The kitchen held its wood-burning cookstove, a tall cupboard, a wash stand, a drop-leaf extension table, and a set of six wonderfully sturdy and comfortable kitchen chairs. There meals were cooked and eaten. On Saturday nights, and not infrequently through the week, the round galvanized iron wash tub was filled and refilled for bathing. A pump lifted bath and laundry water from a cistern under the back porch. Drinking and cooking water had to be carried from the 80-foot deep well that Father had had drilled down into the limestone rock, but it was near the house.

A hearty Round Oak stove, rocking chairs, a stand, and Mother's organ crowded the small front living room. When the fall housecleaning time came, the floor coverings were taken up. The first replacement was a layer, or rather several layers, of newspapers. Mother then called for a supply of fresh wheat straw from the recent threshing, and spread it evenly about. After that the wall-to-wall rag carpet, cleaned and beaten, was tacked back in place with the aid of a carpet-stretching device.

To prevent winter winds from whistling under the floors, Father at about Thanksgiving time would set stakes about a foot away from the foundation sills and place wide boards against the stakes. The intervening space he packed tightly with strawy manure from the horse stables—a simple procedure that saved many cords of wood.

Extremes of cold marked few of our winters. Father often noted the weather in his diary. He recorded a bit of exceptional winter in 1899:

Feb. 7. Hauled ice. Zero
Feb. 8. Hauled sawdust. 14 below zero.
Feb. 9. Hauled sawdust. 20 below zero.
Feb. 13. Stayed by the fire. 21 below Zero.

In return for helping to fill Shelly Shanks's icehouse with ice from Hog Creek and sawdust for its insulation, we had a generous share of the ice—enough for iced tea, lemonade, and occasional ice cream all summer.

With an eye for shade and ornament, and for practical considerations too, soon after acquiring the farm Father set trees around the dooryard. He planted pears, apples, peaches, plums, and cherries, along with a handsome catalpa at the corner and a flourishing hickory by the well. A fine black walnut grew to spread its branches over the woodshed. Across from the graveled lane he set maples and basswood. North of the house a generous and convenient garden plot was bordered by rhubarb and horseradish, along with tiger lilies, striped grass, golden glow, and other perennials. At the far end of the garden, a proper distance from the house, stood a neat, white privy.

We had no lawn mower then, but whenever the blue grass sward grew high, Father mowed it with a scythe. When a neighbor youth, Frank Runser, acquired a camera, complete with tripod, black cloth, and developing equipment, he came one day to make a picture of the place. Father and Mother donned their second-best clothes, and I was in full summer regalia of cap, shirtwaist, and knee pants, with a pet lamb named

Dandy to complicate the pose. We stood in the yard by the old house. Today that picture is valuable to me.

Once a week, usually on Saturday afternoon, Doc, the roan driving horse, was hitched to the buggy and we drove to Ada. About five miles from the farm, this pleasant village was our mail address and shopping center. Mother took her basket of eggs and butter to the grocery store to exchange them for coffee, sugar, salt, vanilla, and whatever other supplies the kitchen cupboard needed. Hopefully she had a little balance in bills or silver to put into her purse, or to finance a brief visit to the dry goods store. Father called at the bank and hardware store, and usually was back at the grocery by the time Mother had finished her errands.

No Ada streets were paved until 1906. In spring the mud was usually so deep that one had to wear high overshoes just to descend from the buggy, tie Doc to the hitching rack, and make it to the sidewalk.

One urgent item in town had been to call at the post office, but about 1898 or 1899 that became unnecessary. Rural Free Delivery came to the farm. Without going to town we could receive mail every day except Sundays and holidays. Letters that reached Ada on Monday were delivered on the same day or the next instead of lying in the General Delivery pigeon holes until Saturday. Letters were frequent because both Father and Mother wrote regularly to relatives and to a few old friends. Soon a daily newspaper was ordered. We felt then that we were in contact with all the world. The mail carrier, John Kanode, followed his route along the Kenton-Lima pike, the south boundary of the farm, and we had to walk only a quarter of a mile to the mail box. The daily paper assured that there always was mail;

we never found the box empty unless, as occasionally happened, we forgot about a holiday.

Those were fast-moving times as the nineteenth century rolled toward its close and the twentieth began. Hardly had we begun to take the R.F.D. for granted than we had a telephone. Father and fifteen neighbors in 1901 formed a telephone company. Father ordered a carload of poles from his brother, Uncle Oren, who was a lumberman in northern Michigan. The company members set up the poles, bought equipment, and had it installed. Our wooden box, complete with bell, receiver, transmitter, and crank, was screwed to the living room wall.

The company was divided into two party lines, eight families on each. The Colliflower family at Huntersville, the hamlet a mile east of us, agreed to operate the "central." John Colliflower was an invalid, unable to work, so his wife and three bright daughters welcomed the employment.

Our ring was "two short." We could call anyone on our line by cranking the appropriate signal—a long and two shorts for Runsers, three shorts for Shanks's, two long for Powells—and anyone on the other line by giving their name to Central. A year or so later our central was connected to the Ada system, and we could also make social or business calls to town. Mostly these were business calls, for we had few social acquaintances there and not many people in town had yet put telephones in their houses.

The telephone line did much to consolidate our community. It brought endless delight to the lonesome farm women, who talked to their hearts' content, sometimes to the high anger of a man in a hurry.

13

Prices were improving a little as the nineties passed. So was the farm. Father was building up the soil by systematic rotation of crops and liberal manuring. He enclosed the fields with strong fences so that livestock could be pastured anywhere, using old-fashioned split rails as long as enough could be found, then building with wire. Tile drainage ditches made the wet corners more productive. In June 1895 the mortgage was paid off, and that fall the splendid new barn was built.

"Raised barn with 28 men. Very windy," the diary noted on October 19. Seventy-two feet long and thirty-six wide, the barn provided warm shelter for the animals, and had high mows in which to store hay, tight bins for wheat and oats, and watering tanks kept filled by the windmill over the well by the house. The total cash cost was $691.12. After eighty years the barn still stands straight and proudly firm.

To pay off a mortgage, improve the farm, and build a fine new barn in the 1890s had taken good planning, careful economy, excellent management, and much hard work. Father never wasted either materials or time. He observed without quoting it the Poor Richard maxim that Uncle Ed had written in my little autograph album: "Lost time is never found." When he worked, and that was most of the time, he tried to make every move and every minute count. When he rested at noon and night, he relaxed. And when he took a vacation, which few farmers did in those years, he devoted himself to enjoyment and rest.

One of those vacations, a trip to northern Michigan in 1899, was the longest since he had bought the farm. The hired man was left at the log house to look after the

14

stock and keep up the work. After we reached Toledo by train, the steamship *Seeandbee* took us aboard at the Maumee River wharf. "Gosh! It's bigger than our barn!" Father exclaimed at first sight of the boat. We had a stateroom to ourselves and ate meals in the big dining room. "First call for dinner!," the steward's shout, for years remained a part of our household language. At Port Huron and Alpena we watched boys dive for pennies that passengers tossed into the water. After a visit at Indian River with Father's uncle, John Carter, and pleasant days fishing and riding the small steamers that plied the nearby streams, we returned by the same route. I was able to tell everyone that we had been out of sight of land on Lake Huron on a boat "bigger'n our barn."

The diary summarized the trip with characteristic brevity: "Aug. 15. Took train for Toledo. From there the steamer to Cheboygan, Mich. Gone two weeks, sightseeing, fishing, boating, hunting." Then came "Sept. 1. Cutting corn." That vacation was over. Others were shorter. In 1904 Father and Mother attended the Louisiana Purchase Exposition at St. Louis.

With all his devotion to work Father found time to be companionable and amusing to a small boy. He taught me how to take a length of half-inch willow stick, cut a deep notch at one end, pound until the bark cylinder slipped off, and cut a small slice from the notch to the end. Then, slip the bark back into place and behold! A whistle!

Whistles were for spring. Fiddles came in the fall. Father knew how to make one from a dry section of heavy cornstalk. Carefully he cut two slits from joint to joint, one under each ridge of the shallow gutter that

15

runs along the side of a stalk. Two little pieces from another section were neatly slid under the slit ends to lift and tighten the two "strings." A longer section, from a stalk not so heavy, when similarly prepared became a bow. A touch of rosin helped to make it squeak; if the boy was small enough and his imagination big enough he had a real fiddle.

One rainy afternoon I found him in the woodshed. He had taken down the long, slender strip of hickory that I remembered his asking me never to touch. He had shaved it down with the drawing knife and notched it with his jack knife into a special shape. With a piece of glass and sandpaper he made all the surface perfectly smooth. A stout string, a handful of long splints from a shingle, and I discovered that he had made for me a "reg'lar" Indian bow and arrows.

He and Mother saw that not all my amusements were homemade. When stockings had been hung behind the Round Oak stove on Christmas Eve, I could count on finding that Santa Claus had brought an iron train, rubber boots, candy, jackstones, a new game, and other delights. Father taught me to play his favorite game of checkers and let me beat him often enough to want to try again. That I never became skilled enough to become a real competitor probably disappointed him.

Now you have been introduced, at least partially, to the man who will be moving through the chapters ahead. With the farm well fenced and better drained, with the fields yielding better crops each year, and with the roomy and gleaming, white-painted barn, Father felt that he was well prepared for whatever future years might bring. Even if prices fell again, he knew he could make a living; if they improved, he could expect to get further ahead.

One major item loomed in his plans. On winter days in the woods he was already preparing for that.

Chapter 2

Mother and the Twentieth-Century House

The distance in time from the new barn to the new house was six years. Father and Mother had not likely concerned themselves much with the significance of what the editorial writers were calling the *fin de siècle*. They had merely determined to build a better house as soon as they could afford one, and as the century turned, that time had come.

One did not put up a new house without first knowing what it was to look like, what materials would be needed, and how to get convenience and comfort without extravagance. An Ada architect was invited to prepare plans and specifications and to estimate costs.

While these were being considered, preparations had proceeded in our woods. The forty acres along the north side of the farm were called the "woods," although no dense forest remained. Its trees had provided all the lumber for the barn except for siding and window frames. Enough mature oaks and ash, maple, beech, sycamore, and basswood remained to be harvested into the sturdy house that now, after nearly three-fourths of a century have elapsed, still stands tight and plumb.

After the wintertime morning chores were finished,

19

Father and the hired man shouldered saws and axes and headed for whatever tree had been chosen to supply particular timbers. Father looked first to see which way the tree should fall. He and the hired man seized the long, crosscut saw and worked vigorously until they had cut from eight inches to a foot into the side toward which they intended the tree to topple. One took an ax and chopped out a triangular slice above the saw-cut. That done, they sawed from the other side until the tree began to sway. An iron wedge driven behind the saw might then be enough to send the tree crashing. If not, they sawed farther, watchfully ready to run. A falling tree could perform against expectations by dropping in the wrong direction, or by lurching to one side; or flying splinters might cause injury. No one ever got hurt while Father was superintending the job.

Branches were quickly trimmed from the fallen tree, sawed or chopped into sixteen-inch lengths, and piled in cords. When well dried they would be hauled to the woodshed to fuel the two stoves. All the small brush was stacked in a neat pile. Green brush could be burned right away once a hot enough fire could be started, but usually time was saved by leaving it to dry. The prostrate log was sawed into prescribed lengths. The pungent smells of wet wood, fresh sawdust, and smoke from burning brush, and the sense of accomplishment as order replaced the fallen tree's disarray, joined to make pleasant those days in the woods.

When a good snow had covered solidly frozen ground, the logs were loaded onto a two-horse bobsled. They could be skidded onto a low sled much more easily than loaded onto a wagon. Charley Guider, at his saw-mill half a mile to the south, sawed the logs according to Father's directions into planks and boards. When the lumber was ready, it was brought home and stacked neatly in the barnyard to cure. The boards were placed on heavy blocks more than a foot from the ground, with higher blocks in front so that the slant would carry off rains. Laths were laid between the layers to permit air to circulate. All the rough lumber for the new house came from these lumber piles. Oak boards for the interior finishing and flooring were hauled to Ada and smoothed at the planing mill.

One August day in 1901 professional movers jacked up the old log house and with their horse-powered winch inched it forward on rollers into the grassy barnyard. Men with shovels, wheelbarrows, and a horse scoop excavated a basement. Masons built rectangular hollow clay tiles into a foundation, and then the carpenters took over. Mother and Father had looked forward to celebrating the holidays with the new house as a sort of family Christmas present, but that was not to be. The painters were slow, and the varnish they applied to the woodwork still slower to dry. New carpets and furniture arrived late. Not until the twenty-first of January 1902 could the beds be set up and the old house vacated.

No farm in the community, or in the whole county so far as we knew, boasted so modern a home. All through that year friends from miles around called to see the house. Strangers, who said they planned to build, came to look. Mother welcomed them all, and was delighted to display every feature. No doubt the house was, in a sense, to Father and Mother what nowadays would be called a "status symbol." Certainly Mother was proud to have a house as good as anyone else she knew owned, and better than any of our rela-

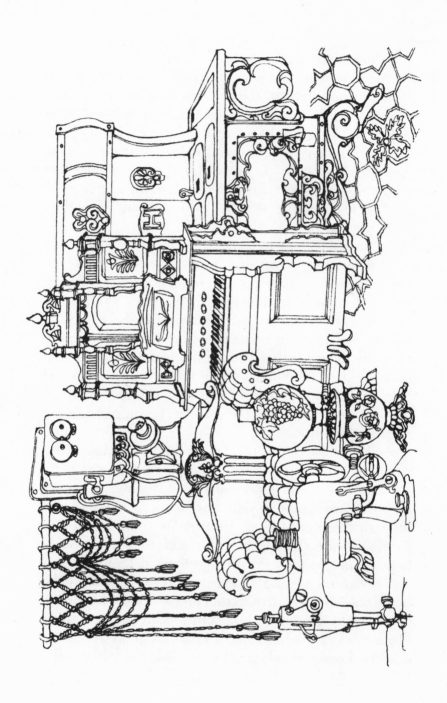

tives occupied; yet she was neither vain nor envious, and would have rejoiced if everyone else had been able to live in such a house. Father, who had no vanity but a modest pride, thought about the practical values and comforts. If he had wanted a status symbol, he could have built a big brick place with columns in front. A substantial, livable house that the family could enjoy, one that added to the value of the farm, and one that was convenient for Mother—those had been his objectives.

When Mother took visitors around, she pointed out that except in the kitchen there was no stove. Bronzed radiators connected to the coal-burning, hot water furnace in the basement that heated the rooms. A new range gleamed in the kitchen, where hot and cold water could be drawn from faucets into the white-enameled sink. The bathroom held a claw-footed tub and a porcelain basin. People were impressed by the two-way cupboard between the kitchen and dining room; everyone thought that was ingenious, as they did the dumbwaiter that saved steps up and down from the basement. Upstairs she showed them the four bedrooms, each with a generous closet, and downstairs the living room, parlor, and bedroom with two closets. The roof, she remarked, was slate; and all could see the roofed porches front and back.

A fireplace in the living room connected into the furnace chimney. The "mantel and grate" had cost $78.07. I suppose Father thought the fireplace would not only save a little coal, but might bring a dividend in pleasant memories of his boyhood home. Unhappily, something was wrong with the chimney, and the fireplace could never be made to work.

Electricity had not yet reached so far out into the country. In the old house, and for some years in the new one, simple kerosene lamps were lit when darkness fell. Mother had wicks to trim, lamps to fill and lamp chimneys to wash almost daily. When an improved kerosene device came along, called from its shape the "Angle Lamp," one of them hung for a few years from the living room ceiling. Later, an acetylene gas system was installed. Acetylene was purchased in drums full of small charcoal-like lumps. A machine located on a cellar ledge mixed it with water to form the gas, which flowed through pipes to the rooms above. The bright, white light reached all corners. No longer did Father have to light an extra lamp when he wanted to work at his desk. Mother rejoiced that she no longer had to trim wicks, fill lamps, and wash the fragile chimneys. The acetylene system was probably more dangerous than we realized; houses were known to have been blown up by it. Father knew there was danger, and saw that all the rules and warnings were rigidly followed.

Individual electric systems, powered by gasoline engines, came along somewhat later. The new house had to wait, however, for nearly thirty years before highline electricity brought its convenient light and power.

Winter work in the woods continued for a while after the new house was finished, and more lumber went to Guider's sawmill. This was used for an extension at the rear of the barn that doubled the floor space and made room for feeding larger numbers of cattle and sheep. With that done, Father considered the building plant complete, except for two more jobs that soon were accomplished. One was the destruction and removal of the old log barn and straw shed. The other was to erect a new house for Mother's chickens.

Once it had been finished and furnished, the house was definitely Mother's domain. No question ever rose about who was head of the family. That was Father, not merely because he was masculine but because he was confident of his judgment on major matters. Mother apparently never rebelled against his authority. He could be decisive, but he was gentle and reasonable, too. If they ever quarreled, they must have done so in privacy, for I never heard heated or harsh words between them. If they disagreed, they talked the problem out quietly. Father gave her no orders about running the house. She planned her work, got it done as best she could, and saw that the meals were ready on time.

Good cheer came easily and naturally to Mother. About five feet four, black-haired, her gray eyes seemed to twinkle as she spoke and smiled. When she was approaching seventy, an old acquaintance applied an adjective to her that would have described her quite as well in earlier years, too; she was, he said, "chipper."

Mother's parents, John and Mary Wheeler, had emigrated from Lincolnshire, England, to Canada in 1855. Her two brothers and two of her four sisters were English-born. Soon after Mother's birth near Ingersoll, Ontario, in 1863, the family moved to the neighborhood of Flushing, Michigan, a few miles from Flint. Both her father and mother died soon afterward, and much of her childhood had been spent in a brother's family. She was hardly grown when she accompanied a married older sister to Ohio. There, until her marriage, she had been the Bowling Green merchant's "hired girl." If she had not already learned the arts of housekeeping, that experience gave her a thorough training.

Proud as she was of the new house, and much as she enjoyed its conveniences as compared with the crowded old one, Mother found little difference in her weekly routines. Monday was still washday, and no automatic equipment had come to do that indispensable task. The tub and washboard, a hand-operated washing machine, and the hand-cranked wringer had not changed. After the clothes had been dried on the outdoor line, the ironing was to be done, with old-fashioned flatirons heated on the kitchen stove. Beds had to be made, and dishes had to be washed and dried. Weekly, the accumulated cream, skimmed from the gallon crocks, was placed in the barrel churn to be jostled into butter. An annual or semi-annual general house-cleaning she regarded as essential, as she did other occasional jobs.

One of the oldtime economies—or maybe it was by her preference—continued long into the new century. It began when an open-topped barrel was placed on a low, slightly slanted platform under the walnut tree back of the woodshed. Once a year a layer of straw was packed into the bottom, and the barrel was filled with wood ashes. Now and then a pail of water was poured over the ashes. (Our buckets were always called pails.) A small iron kettle sat under the edge of the slanted platform, and into it dripped the lye that drained from the bottom of the barrel.

Meantime, inside the woodshed a five-gallon earthen jar accumulated cracklings and any surplus fat from the kitchen. At a time when the quantities of lye and fat appeared suitable, Mother directed that the big kettle be hung. Half a globe in itself, the round kettle was suspended at the edge of the woodyard from a triangular plank tripod. Under it a fire was started, and plenty of additional fuel lay close by. From that point Mother took over and asked for no further aid. I cannot fully describe the process, but at its end she had a generous supply of slippery, brown soft soap that she used thereafter on washdays and in the dishpan. The procedure was quite unlike that of buying packages of detergents or soap flakes, and the clothes came clean, too.

The larger house, though more convenient, must have demanded more sweeping and dusting than did the old one. Nor did it eliminate for Mother such chores as patching and mending clothing and socks. Farm work could wear and tear. With the aid of her sewing machine she made many of her own dresses and shirts for Father and me. As a small boy, I always had warm woolen mittens that she had knitted for winter wear.

Before spring had advanced far, Mother had saved up 120 choice eggs, or had bought them from a poultry breeder if she had decided to try a new strain, and had set them in her kerosene-heated incubator in the basement. For three weeks she watched to keep the temperature steady at 102.5°, and every other day she turned the eggs, as hens were known to do. The twenty-first day brought the excitement of seeing the shells pipped and the more vigorous chicks making their way into their new world. She probably never obtained a full hatch, but likely a hundred or more of the babies cheeped for feed and care, first in the kitchen and then soon in a warm brooder house outside. The young roosters were expected to grow up into Sunday dinners and the pullets into producers of eggs for cooking and money for Mother.

Although she was always delighted to collect a bit of cash from her poultry ventures, she was never dependent upon them. When she needed money, Father never hesitated to supplement her supply. He knew she was as frugal as he was, and that none would be wasted.

Despite all the work she did, Mother took it for granted as her share in the partnership, and seldom complained about it. She knew how to relax, too. She could turn to the telephone and, if the line was not busy, chat for a while with one of the neighbor women. (She could not sit down to use the telephone. For no good reason the instruments were fastened to the wall at stand-up height; otherwise, the hardworking farm wives might have enjoyed a little more ease.) Now and then her rest came at the old reed organ, and later at her piano, where she would run through a part of her small repertoire or play a few favorite hymns. She often sang while at work, usually old ballads that she had learned as a child. One of her regulars was an old temperance song whose refrain was "Have courage, my boy, to say No." That may have been an admonition to her growing son.

Father probably realized that the daily household routine could grow wearisome, no matter how cheerfully it was performed. Few years went by when he did not put her on the train for a visit with their relatives in Wood County, or with her brothers, sisters, and old friends in Michigan. One year—this was in 1897, while we still lived in the old house—she took the youngster in hand and made an excursion to Buffalo and Niagara Falls. She visited a cousin, but the occasion was the annual encampment of the Grand Army of the Republic, to which her two brothers belonged. It was made notable by a glimpse of the president of the United States, William McKinley, as his carriage passed in the parade. She greatly admired McKinley, especially because of his devotion to his invalid wife. Tears streamed down her face on the day in September 1901 when she came from the house to say that someone had telephoned news that McKinley had been shot and was not expected to live. She could not understand why anyone could want to destroy a man who was so kind.

A change of scene could be worth considerable effort. One day at dinner, when I was about eleven, she announced the she and I were going to make an excursion to Gauley Bridge to see the mountains in West Virginia.

We drove old Doc next afternoon the eleven miles to Kenton and arranged for his stay in a livery barn. At the railroad station so large a crowd had gathered that we wondered how all could get on the train. We waited impatiently until the long, long string of day coaches pulled in, and the crowd scrambled aboard. We found a seat together and stowed away the basket and the box of fried chicken, sandwiches, and pie that she had packed. All night we rode through darkness, except as an occasional town blinked by and as the train was shuttled around the rail yards in Columbus. Mother giggled at the antics of some of the more boisterous passengers and visited with a new acquaintance or so, until we settled down to sleep in the rather less than comfortable seats.

The next morning we found Gauley Bridge—hardly more than a bare, sooty railroad station in the midst of the West Virginia mountains. The sun had not yet risen over the steep slopes to the east. We watched the shadows fall lower on the equally high opposite ridge, strolled around a bit, and ignored the hawkers with their balloons, pennants, and pop. Within an hour we had seen the sights. The rest of the day we simply watched people and stared at the unfamiliar wooded mountain sides. We had never seen mountains before, and that was what Mother had come to behold.

After the sun had dropped behind the ridge to the west, we climbed aboard with our fellow excursionists and rode back to Kenton through another grimy night. Old Doc whinnied happily as he greeted us and trotted briskly back home again.

"My cooking is pretty good," Father said grinning as we began to tell him of our adventures. "But," he added, with a pat on Mother's shoulder, "I like yours better."

She had lifted her eyes up unto the hills.

Chapter 3

Hired Men Were Characters

Completion of the new house brought one big relief to Mother. She no longer had to cook and wash for hired men, and evenings could be enjoyed in family privacy. Until that time, Father employed single men, and there was no alternative to keeping them in the house. Most of them were worthy of the privilege, and when they moved on they left behind them entertaining memories that became embedded in the family lore and speech.

After the old house was empty, it was moved to a space north of the orchard and equipped with its own cistern and outbuildings. Thereafter, married men with families could be employed. Father was seldom without an assistant. By feeding carloads of cattle or sheep in winter, he could afford to provide a man with work all year. With another man on the farm to see that chores were done and animals cared for, he could when he chose be absent for an afternoon or a week for business or pleasure.

With a reputation for fair dealing and for his willingness to work alongside his help at any task, Father usually had his choice from among those who wanted full-time farm jobs. Few who worked for him were of the ruder sort; he knew how to select individuals who were tolerable company, clean, and mannerly enough to be acceptable.

Not many emergencies occurred around the farm, because Father was a man who planned. He replenished supplies of nails, rivets, repair parts, flour, and other essentials. Affairs seldom were interrupted for want of a nail, nor of a horse or horseshoe either.

Such an occasion did arise one midweek in the midst of the busiest summer season. Mother discovered that we were nearly out of coal oil—we seldom called it kerosene then—and coal oil was a necessity for lights after dark and for the oil stove. A dinner table council discussed the problem. Should someone take time to make an off-schedule trip to town? Or should Mother cook on the hot wood stove and burn candles for a few nights?

The hired man then was Oak Pringle, a fine young man from Findlay, some thirty miles north. He contributed a sage question. "Lew," he said, "when you get coal oil again, why don't you buy a barrel of it? Then, when you run out you'll have some."

Even today I seldom lay in a six-months' supply of razor blades or shaving soap, or a future store of household requirements, without thinking of Oak's "When you run out, you'll have some." In time Father did buy a 50-gallon tank for coal oil and surely never ran out thereafter.

Oak had been about sixteen when he came to the farm, and he stayed three or four years. When he returned to Findlay, he became a successful blacksmith, with his shop in a prominent corner back of the courthouse. In later years, when driving through Findlay, we usually stopped to see him. A time came when the shop could not be found. Oak had abandoned it to become janitor of a school building. "Blacksmithing isn't what it used to be," he explained when we finally located him. His dancing dark eyes always held their friendly gleam; his white teeth and black mustache still adorned his delighted smile whenever we looked him up. More than a quarter-century after he left us, when Father died, Oak was one of those to whom we sent a telegram, and he came for the funeral. He had never quite ceased to be one of the family.

We looked upon Frank Spurrier, an early successor to Oak, as an intellectual, a real phenomenon among hired men. His prime winter night amusement was to solve problems in higher algebra and trigonometry. After supper he would sit down with a mathematics book at hand, a long yellow tablet, and a sharply pointed pencil. With the tablet on his knee, he would figure steadily until the clock struck nine. That was always bedtime for everyone. Whether he worked the problems solely for fun, or had dreams of a higher career, we never asked nor did he say. We assumed that he solved the problems correctly. The yellow sheets were impressively covered with his neat and orderly figures, and Frank was too methodical to have set down incorrect solutions. His handwriting was practically perfect copybook Spencerian script. I have a specimen of it yet, in the copy of Milton's *Paradise Lost* that he gave to me on my eighth birthday. Even then, the text was a little over my head.

Frank subscribed to the *Review of Reviews*, *World's Work*, and to Orrison Swett Marden's then famous *Success* magazine. Father read these, too, and after Frank went his way continued the *Review of Reviews* for several years.

He worked for exactly twelve months, and took no penny of his wages until the day he left; then he drew the full year's pay upon which he and Father had agreed in advance. His check was for $126—$10.50 a month, room, washing, and board.

Four or five years after he had gone away to parts unknown, we heard that Frank had purchased a ten-acre tract on the edge of Ada. Upon it he built, by his own careful workmanship, a small cottage where he lived until the sudden end of his life. He planted his acres to vegetables, strawberries, melons, and small fruit and made his living by selling the produce. One day a Pennsylvania "fast line" train struck him, and his body was found at the side of the tracks near his home. Had he deliberately thrown himself in front of the train, or had he not noticed its approach? That mystery and others about Frank Spurrier were never solved.

The first hired man to occupy the old house, Marshall McElroy, suited Father probably better than any other in the whole series; hired men were a series, because the best of them eventually went on to better jobs, and the inferior ones achieved discontent wherever they worked. Marshall stayed for three or four years. He was a small, wiry man who knew how things should be done and did them faithfully. His wages were $260 a year, house, garden, some meat, and the milk from one cow. On this he maintained his wife, three small daughters, and a baby son.

Marshall's quiet efficiency and pleasant manners

won Father's praise. He chewed quantities of scrap tobacco, as did most of the later hired men. Smoking around the farm was not encouraged; in the barn or in a dry grainfield it was too dangerous. Besides, a chewer could expectorate without stopping work, but a pipe-smoker was always having to suspend the labors of both hands to renew his fire. The farm never had a cigarette problem; only town dudes smoked "coffin nails."

The McElroys left to move to a Cleveland suburb, where Marshall took a factory job. His successor, burly Terry Nash, was a good worker, but his departure at the end of a year was not regretted. His manners were rough and his language coarse. Father disapproved of profanity and vulgarity. If a man released a sudden outburst over some momentary vexation, Father was not likely to say anything, but his silence and his own example usually discouraged repetition of offensive words.

Occasionally an extra hand was employed to help through the busiest harvest season. One of these was Ben Warner who, as a single man, slept in our house and ate at our table. It was Ben who explained to me that if one planted a silver dollar in the garden, it would grow into a plant bearing dozens of dimes. Just at that interval I happened not to be owning a silver dollar. The idea sounded so productive that I besought Father to lend me one, promising to return in due time at least ten, maybe eleven or twelve dimes.

His reply was to send me for an ear of corn and a potato. After pointing out the eye of the potato and the germ in a grain of corn, he said, "A dollar is not alive, and it has no germ as does a seed." He finally convinced me that I had been teased, and then explained how a dollar could be made to grow some interest if saved and properly invested.

Ben teased me with other improbable stories, but the tables eventually were turned, though not by me. My cousin, Inez, came for a visit. She was the daughter of Aunt Emma, Mother's oldest sister, who had married an Oklahoma pioneer. Having entered Oklahoma too early for the oil boom, Uncle Jared ran a livery barn in Guthrie. Among the five Wheeler sisters he was reputed to be the meanest husband any of them had acquired.

Inez was then about nineteen, friendly and pleasant, wearing all the attractive bloom of a well-matured young lady. Sex appeal was not then a familiar term, but with curves, complexion, and charm, Inez had it.

One pleasant July Sunday morning Ben was seen washing his fairly new buggy. Before noon it shone with a special splendor. His horse was curried to the last hair. He had gone over the harness so thoroughly that every strap gleamed and every buckle glittered. After the usual generous Sunday noontime dinner, he hitched the horse to the buggy and tied it under the maple tree at the head of the lane. Dressed in his own best, he passed through the kitchen where Inez was helping Mother wash the dishes, found various occasions to busy himself in and out of the house, and sat for a time with Father on the shady south porch. At four o'clock the impatient horse and shining buggy were still hitched at the lane gate.

I was dimly aware of an unusual tension. Mother appeared to be uneasy. Then, casually sauntering into the back yard, Inez began kicking a green pear across the grass until she was some distance from the house. Suddenly Ben managed to pass as though en route to his buggy, and spoke to her. Still kicking at the pear, she shook her head and said something inaudible to us in reply. Ben untied his horse, jumped into the buggy, and drove rapidly down the road. Mother visibly relaxed.

"I kicked that pear out there on purpose," I overheard Inez tell her. "I knew he wanted to ask me to go out with him, and so I gave him a chance to find out that I wouldn't."

I was impressed by the curious nature of feminine ways.

By the time Clint Hinkle moved into the old house, I had grown big enough to share in most of the farm jobs. One wet summer the weather had prevented the usual early cultivation, and grass was growing in the rows of a 14-acre corn field. Father hated all weeds; weeds in growing corn he considered to be absolutely intolerable. So the field had to be hoed, and there was not too much time to get that done before the hay harvest.

A combination of wiles developed. Father had recently heard Clint and me talking about chocolate drops, the cream-centered kind of which in those years one could buy more for a nickel than he ought to eat at any one time. Neither Clint nor I could recall ever having had more than a nickel's worth at once of this desirable confection; we wondered how many one really could eat and declared that we would be willing to find out. Thereupon Father offered us what may have been the only serious bet he ever made. He proposed to wager us a quarter's worth of chocolate drops *apiece* that we could not finish hoeing those fourteen acres, and do a thorough job, within the number of days he specified. Clint and I finished the field in time and collected the chocolates. I have never since cared much for them.

Maybe it was not entirely fair to Clint that I had a very special incentive—a sort of side bet. The urge to put words on paper had become severe, and I wanted a typewriter. No store in Ada handled typewriters, but I learned from a mail-order dealer that a rebuilt L. C. Smith could be bought for $35. Though I was willing to expend all my current store of cash, the amount fell far short of $35. I had discussed the matter with Father. He promised nothing, but did agree that if Clint and I should get that cornfield hoed on schedule he would give some consideration to means of acquiring the typewriter. Desiring anxiously that his consideration be favorable, I hoed faster than ever before, and crowded Clint to keep up with me. When the job was done, Father considered, as he had promised to do. He looked over the mail-order literature and wrote out a check for the entire $35.

Other hired men came and went. One of Harry Marling's stipulations was that he should be permitted once a week to use the horse and buggy to go for his groceries. Invariably upon his return he would report, with a solemn smile, "Well, I got back!" That became a part of our household language.

Edward, who worked one year from March until winter, was a Negro. Unmarried, his mother kept the tenant house for him. No one remarked adversely about his being hired, although he was the only black man in the vicinity. He was respected for his willingness and good cheer, and admired for his physical strength. Complimented one day for lifting something that ordinarily took two men, he remarked that he could lift a horse. We had to see about that. He selected old Nora, a member of the draft team, a solidly built mare who weighed more than 1400 pounds. Edward stooped under the gentle old mare until his head was between her forelegs, and when he felt that her body was balanced he raised up. Sure enough, in a moment all of her four feet were off the ground, dangling in thin air. Edward delightedly repeated the act when visitors expressed interest.

Then there was Marve. Marvin Phillips had barely reached McGuffey's Fourth Reader when he quit going to our district school. Lessons had little interest for him, though he could draw fascinating pictures of traction engines. His ambition then had been to become the engineer with a threshing outfit. That desire he satisfied. But after he had married Lillie Hunsicker, a hearty, good-looking, and gracious neighborhood girl, he felt the need for more continuous employment than the few weeks that threshing provided, and welcomed the small but steady wages, along with the house and extras, that farm work offered.

By today's standards, the farmhand's lot sixty years ago would seem to have been hard and unreasonable. The hours were long, though not from "sun to sun" as may have been true in earlier times. From March into November, the months when most of the field work was done, the normal schedule called for man and team to be in the field by seven in the morning, with breakfast and chores out of the way before that hour. At noon an hour—often an hour and a half—provided time for dinner and a short rest. The coffee break had not then been invented; but during hot and tiresome work, no one objected to stopping long enough to swig a cool drink from the earthen jug that usually went along to the fields, and then to sit down for ten or fifteen minutes ease. The work day ended at six o'clock unless, as rarely happened, a harvest task could be finished with a few minutes more work or another load of hay could be brought in before rain came. Then the evening chores followed—milking the cows, feeding the hogs, and seeing that the horses were comfortable. The rule was to spend ten hours in the field and do chores before and after. Except to give the livestock necessary care, no Sunday work was required. Father did none himself on Sundays other than to give the animals their weekly salt.

Even with room and board, or the house with other perquisites that were a part of the deal, the wages to farmhands before World War I look pitiably small. Still, they compared not too unfavorably with compensations in other fields. The factory worker, store clerk, or newspaper reporter who earned $12 to $15 a week was doing fairly well, even with house rent or room and board to pay. Men sought the farm jobs, and Father's reputation gave him a choice among the men who were available.

Without exception, his hired men were faithful and responsible. None tended to "soldier" on the job, even though the boss was away or the job was in a back field where none could see. None neglected the livestock. Nevertheless, Father became convinced that men would work better and be happier if they had an incentive beyond their fixed wages.

And so, he rented the farm to Marve Phillips "on the thirds." In return for his year's work, Marve could count on receiving a third of the year's receipts, less a third of cash costs for fertilizers, threshing bills, or other specified outlays. The better he did the job, the more carefully he looked after the feeding stock, the larger his pay would be. If he saved enough to buy horses and machinery of his own, he could hope eventually to rent "on the halves." By such steps up the agricultural ladder thousands of American hired men became owners of their own farms.

Father enjoyed Marve's tenure, both because he was reliable and because he could joke and take a joke. He had an extraordinary facility for finding objects—pocket knives, coins, arrowheads—that were turned up in the fields. He was slope-shouldered and habitually walked in a posture that was rather less than erect. One day Father, half serious and half jocular, gave him a short lecture.

"Marve, why don't you stand up straight? Throw back your shoulders and stick out your chest! Why walk with your eyes on the ground all the time? Why don't you look up, instead of down?"

Marve grinned as he delivered his answer. "Lew, I never found nothin' yet when I was lookin' up."

Chapter 4

Self-sufficient— Almost, But Not Quite

The first families to pioneer the new lands had to be almost completely self-sufficient. They had little that could be sold for cash or bartered for goods. Not many things were available to buy even if they had money. Their successors on the farms already cleared, such as Father and Mother, had in a way inherited a tradition; nor had the necessity for economy vanished. Prudence and thrift demanded that the family should produce as many of its requirements as possible, and should make use of what came to hand.

This imposed no hardship. The year around Mother expected to place three meals a day on the table. She did, and we found them good. Most of her culinary resources derived from within a few rods of the kitchen, but they were highly varied, abundant, and she knew what to do with them. Her three meals were never late nor did anyone ever leave the table hungry. Although meat and potatoes formed staple ingredients of our hearty diet, she made good use of her many other resources.

The garden was basic. In late winter the plot was covered liberally with rich soil stimulants from the horse stables. As soon as the earth was warmed and not too damp, it was plowed, harrowed thoroughly, and smoothed. Stakes and strings marked out the rows, and, along each at the appropriate times, the seeds and plants were placed. Within short weeks the first harvests would yield radishes, leaf lettuce, and green peas. In due time the beets and carrots, string, pole, and lima beans, and the early potatoes were ready.

From a greenhouse in town we had bought cabbage and sweet potato plants, and dozens of tomato plants. These yielded table supplies until into winter, as did the parsnips. Before even the first radish could be pulled, the perennial rhubarb had responded to the sun. Some of the long and tender stalks had been snapped off, their big green leaves lopped, and their sour succulence turned into sauce or baked into pies. Those who nowadays expect to find almost every item, regardless of the local season, displayed daily in the supermarkets will not fully appreciate the pleasant anticipation with which we awaited the first dish from each garden crop nor the delight with which we relished it, knowing always that each had its own season and that when that passed we would have to wait most of the year until another summer.

More than to anything else we looked forward to the ripening of the roasting ears. Two rows of sweet corn were planted, then ten days or two weeks later another two, and finally a third pair, thus to extend the season as long as possible. Out of the garden and into the pot with only time enough to remove the husks, the gleaming ears came hot to the table ready to be bathed in butter and eaten in what approached ecstasy. We enjoyed them usually at least once a day while they

44

lasted, and didn't mind having them for both dinner and supper.

If enough ears were available, as usually they were, Mother sliced the grains from a considerable number and spread them on a cloth in the sun, or in the store room, under a mosquito netting to keep off the flies. When the corn was fully dehydrated, she hung it up in a cotton bag to be saved for winter, when we liked it only a little less than when gnawed fresh from the cobs.

Rival to the roasting ear weeks and coming a bit sooner, strawberry time enriched the early summer. Each spring Father set out new rows. From these the blossoms were pinched off to allow the plants to give all their attention to growing. Late the next May their modest white blossoms peeped from under the leaves and gave way to promising green berries that soon—and none too soon for us—turned beautifully scarlet and crimson. The first ripe quarts adorned enough biscuit-dough shortcake to provide each of us with firsts and seconds—the cake well soaked in enticing red juice and enhanced by as much cream or milk as one cared to apply. Until the berry vines ceased their fruiting we reveled daily at dinner and supper and often breakfast over generous bowls of the ever-delicious berries and the satisfying goodness of Mother's shortcakes. Those underprivileged persons who know of strawberry shortcake only as the hotel species of dry pastry, six hard berries, and a dab of synthetic whipped cream can form no idea of the genuine and perfect creation.

The acre and a half of apple orchard Father had set out soon after he bought the farm brought him disappointment. He was fond of apples, and had memories of those he had enjoyed in boyhood days. The nursery that had supplied the trees evidently had been careless or unreliable, for few turned out to be the varieties he had ordered. Then, by the time the few good ones began to bear fruit, the years had arrived when orchard insects became so plentiful that without frequent spraying much of the fruit was imperfect. Proper and timely application of sprays interfered so much with more important farm work that Father decided to leave the orchard to its fate, which ultimately was to be an acre and a half of uprooted trees.

Nevertheless, by early July the Red Astrachans, handsomely greenish with red stripes, were ready for Mother to turn into pies, cobblers, and apple sauce. A few later trees bore good cooking apples, which she patiently pared and cut out the damaged portions. "Too good to throw away," she said.

Pumpkins became plentiful by September, for they grew abundantly along with the corn in a nearby field. Every week until well into winter she baked pumpkin pies along with her others.

In addition to the small garden north of the house, an acre or more in some nearby field was set apart as the "truck patch." Here the major supply of potatoes grew, along with extra rows of sweet corn, tomatoes, late cabbage, cucumbers, and muskmelons. Freshly ripened tomatoes came to the table from summer until frost, and so many went into Mason jars that the reserve was never quite exhausted. Through the winter stewed tomatoes were on the menu almost daily. We did not know about vitamins then, or buy orange juice, so perhaps the tomatoes provided for a bodily need of which we were not aware. Anyway, we liked them; and Mother's tomato soup is a cherished memory.

One highly special spring treat in occasional years and an every-year-after-frost treat marked minor gustatory peaks. Not every spring, but one misty morning around May's first week I might have a few hours to wander around the nearby woodlands, ours and others. And I might—just might—discover a patch of morels. These sponge-shaped mushrooms are little known outside the Midwest. If I found only two or three under one tree, the search was prolonged until I had a hatful. One never carried a basket or a bucket when searching for mushrooms. Only by luck and persistence could one discover them, even in locations where in other springs they may have been plentiful. And a hatful was as many as were likely to be found in one morning. Moreover, a hatful could be enough to fill a fair-sized bowl after Mother had washed them and fried them in butter— enough for all three of us. No commercial, cellar-grown mushroom nor any other can as much as suggest the heavenly excellence of the morel. If the ambrosia consumed by the gods on Olympus was half as delicious, those super-beings lived high.

The autumn after-frost treat was certain. Though it grew in the garden, to our knowledge it had never been sown or planted, and was not actually cultivated. After the sweet corn, early potatoes, and such had been used up, a sprawling, fuzzy green plant emerged and spread lazily over the ground. Small, yellowish blossoms could be noted in August, and by September these had transformed into small Japanese lantern-like pendants. Inside each of these a tomato-shaped fruit formed, greenish at first, richly yellow when ripe. Its skin was tomato-smooth and its contents tomato-pulpy, the seeds soft. Botanically and correctly the name was husk tomato. We knew them as ground-cherries.

The correct destination for ground-cherries had to be pies, and that was where Mother placed them. The dearth of suitable adjectives inhibits any attempt to describe, or even to hint at, the delicate and unique flavor of ground-cherry pie. Flavors refuse to be defined exactly, described precisely, counted, or measured in minute terms. Even the best apple pie, one of the world's great inventions, can be improved by the addition of ground-cherries. Angel-food cake is supposed to be so-called because of its fitness for higher beings. With greater appropriateness ground-cherry pie could be called angel-food pie.

Long after the Golden Years, when a multimillion farm readership was available, I proposed creation of a Society for the Promotion of More Ground-cherry Pie. The response was negligible. Only a few dozen readers replied. So I learned that even though nothing else in my farming youth was distinctive, I must have been among the rare individuals to have tasted ground-cherry pie, not only once but many times and over several years.

The morels were about the only food product we obtained from the "wild," except for an occasional rabbit shot in winter and elderberries. Neglected fence rows and swampy places in the neighborhood commonly held clumps of elder bushes from which the clustered berries could easily be gathered. In a purple, juicy pie they were acceptable although by no means a favored flavor. A boy, of course, also had to sample a few May apples when they ripened, and try a taste of pawpaws in the fall, but such as these were not to be honored at the table. Edible but not particularly good, they were amusements rather than nutriments.

As summer days passed, the new brood of young chickens feathered out and took on flesh. Meanwhile, the meat stores might be running low. The fried chicken period was about to begin and would last until the birds outgrew the frier stage.

Nowadays when a farm woman decides on chicken for the table she may as likely as not do what her urban sister does—choose at the supermarket the pieces she wants from a counter spread with fowls cut up and ready for the stove; or she may even buy one already cooked. The farmyard poultry flock that scratched for bugs and worms and whatever else might supplement a scattering of grain no longer frequents every homestead along the rural routes. This has something to do with the economy, or with time-saving, or with something else that I can't explain.

One Saturday evening Mother might snatch a couple of the sturdiest cockerels—Plymouth Rock or Rhode Island Red, whichever she was raising that year—off the roost and chuck them into a small coop where they could be collected next morning. Or else an old broomstick with a wire hook on one end was produced next forenoon and the flock invited to an unexpected feed of grain. A deft reach hooked and brought the victims squawking to hand. The nearest male was summoned. He gathered the feet and wingtips in one hand to prevent flopping, laid the head and neck across the woodyard chopping block, and severed the head with a swift stroke of ax or hatchet. Quickly he tossed the bird away so that its final struggles did not bloody his clothing. Another technique was to hold the bird by the head and twirl it rapidly until the neck was broken.

Mother plunged the lifeless bird into a pail of hot water, plucked off the plumage, and with a flaming newspaper singed off the pinfeathers. Then all she had to do was to clean out the interior, cut the carcass into the desired pieces, and cook. That her fried chicken was any better than other good farm cooks could serve might be a rash assertion. Certainly it was superior to that being vended these days by any franchised roadside stand. The chicken itself, moreover, was only number one of the two delights that emerged from the skillet. The other was cream cravy—cream *chicken* gravy—a preparation of *ne plus ultra* merit when poured liberally over a mound of potatoes or even a slice of bread.

The electric refrigerator was far in the future, but from the already-mentioned storage at Shanks's, a half mile north, we had ice enough for special purposes. In time an ice wagon passed the farm twice a week, and then an icebox stood on the back porch and became a necessity theretofore unknown. The special purposes for ice had been to cool tea or lemonade and to make ice cream. While Mother stirred up the ingredients for this delicacy, the boy placed a suitable hunk of ice inside a burlap bag and pounded with ax or maul until all was in small pieces. The ingredients were poured into a metal cylinder that in turn was set down into a wooden, keg-like container to which a crank and gears were attached. Salted ice was packed around the space between cylinder and container, and the boy turned the crank to revolve the paddle that worked inside the cylinder. In time, which always seemed to be needlessly long, the crank turned harder and harder until it could scarcely be budged. More ice and salt were applied as melted water began to flow from the little hole bored for its escape. Finally muscles could no longer move the crank. Mother carefully raised the top to make sure that the contents had reached the proper stage. If so, she pulled out the paddle and set it in a crock or pan, and the cranker rewarded himself by licking off whatever ice cream adhered. Then she packed in more ice and left the freezer until time to serve. The process was more laborious than picking up a quart at the supermarket, but the product, rich with real cream and flavored just right with the vanilla she always used, was all the more esteemed because we did not have it every week.

Milk and its products were never lacking. We kept two cows. Two were necessary. After some ten months of lactation one would "dry up." Until after her calf was born, and a few days longer until her milk was fit to use, she was on vacation while the other remained on duty. Our cows would have won no prizes, but their Jersey ancestry assured rich milk. By making sure that their arid periods never coincided, the daily flow always was adequate. Mother strained the milk each morning and evening into gallon earthen crocks that rested coolly on the wide cellar ledge. Cream was skimmed and kept separately to be used as needed for coffee or cooking, or to be churned into butter whenever enough surplus accumulated. No milk was wasted. A surplus at any time could be allowed to sour and the curds converted into cottage cheese. Mother called it smearcase. Our liberal consumption of butter and cream, which were saleable, exemplified the viewpoint that, though extravagance was not approved, neither was penuriousness. Butter was sold only when we had more than we could use.

Once a week Mother baked bread. For years this came from our own wheat that Father took to the grist mill in Ada, where it was ground into flour for us and middlings and bran for the young pigs. After the grist mill burned down, flour was purchased.

At noon and evening the table almost always displayed a pie, and rare were the times when anyone ignored its presence. Through all the seasons when they were available, Mother canned peaches, raspberries, strawberries, plums, cherries, and apples. She like to buy a bushel of plums—Damsons or Green Gages—or a half bushel of cherries, since the farm did not regularly produce these fruits. She spoke of them as her "pie timber." Also she baked mince pies for which she must have bought the "timber," for I cannot recall her making mincemeat, and soft pies, too—custard, chess, lemon, and chocolate. A tall old earthen jar in the pantry was constantly supplied with ginger snaps or sugar cookies and regularly emptied by you-know-who. Occasionally she made a cake. One kind was filled with chopped hickory nuts or walnuts. More likely it would be the jam cake for which she enjoyed a local celebrity. This was a dark cake whose recipe called for a liberal quantity of strawberry jam, and was iced with chocolate and crowned by hickory nut kernels. One of its unique qualities was that it was supposed to "fall," to collapse in the middle, after leaving the oven.

Most years we raised an ample crop of strawberries

for such worthy purposes as this. Her strawberry jam, spread liberally over a well-buttered slice of the home-baked bread, never ceased to be a favorite snack, and was ever a principle ingredient in my school lunch boxes. If ever our own strawberry patch proved insufficient, she bought two or three bushels to meet the demand for jam.

Next in preference as a spread was crab apple jelly. We had no crab apple trees, but Mother knew who did and bought enough to fill scores of glasses with the gleaming product. From the spreading cucumber vines she collected and canned quarts of pickles.

The basic "meat and potatoes" of our diet never became monotonous. Mother varied her ways of cooking potatoes; they came to the table boiled, with or without jackets, baked, scalloped, fried, creamed, or mashed. Occasionally we swapped quarters of beef with neighbors. A calf for veal, a sheep for mutton, or a lamb were slaughtered once or twice a year.

A sharp cold day in early winter was chosen for re-newing the major pork supply. The proceedings began with setting a blazing fire in the woodyard under the big iron kettle. For the honors of the occasion two of the best shotes had been elected. Shot and bled, each was plunged into and out of a slanted barrel of hot water until the hair was loosened and could be scraped away. Washed, the carcass was hung by the hind feet under a stout tripod to be opened for removing the entrails and then was placed upon a temporary bench to be carved into the usual cuts. These were stored on clean boards in the summer kitchen until thoroughly chilled. The tradi-tional smokehouse we did not have. Hams and shoulders were rubbed with seasoning and painted repeatedly with a "liquid smoke" preparation that cured and preserved them well. Most of the fat was cut away to be rendered into lard. Smaller pieces of meat were ground into sausage, which, after seasoning, was put away in gallon jars.

Sausage, with pancakes made from wheat, buckwheat, or corn meal flour and served with plenty of syrup, gave the cold winter mornings a good start. Breakfast was eaten early, in the winter before the morning chores. Stewed prunes or another fruit began it, followed by a hot cereal, which on most mornings was rolled oats. We called it oatmeal, whatever the box said. Ham and fried eggs, or perhaps fried potatoes, gave us plenty of proteins, fats, carbohydrates and whatever else it took to keep one going until noon. We were too active to have thought of counting calories even had we known such things existed.

With all this diversity of good things that came from the farm itself, we still were not completely self-sufficient. From the grocery store Mother brought rice to boil and make into pudding, and crackers to put into the stewed tomatoes and for other purposes. She bought vanilla and chocolate, white and brown sugar, salt and spices, prunes and lemons, coffee, tea, corn starch, and cereals.

We were organic farmers and ate organic food, although, of course, we were not aware of that fact. The only pesticide used was Paris Green, sprinkled over the potato vines if the Colorado beetles grew too numerous to be picked off by hand and drowned in a can of kerosene. No commercial fertilizer reached the farm before 1912 when Father found that acid phosphate paid well when applied to the wheat ground.

As viewed from this remote distance in time, Mother's routine years of cooking, washing dishes, and doing her housework seem to have been arduous and perhaps dull. She took it all in stride and for granted, as a part of destiny. I never heard her express envy of other women who might have more or work less. She lived until well into her seventy-sixth year.

Chapter 5

The Years Began with Spring

The strands of autumn always reached across the winter and into spring. A forehanded farmer, if weather and work conditions in late fall permitted, had anticipated the busy spring by plowing his sod fields where the summer's hay had grown. The moistening snow and heaving frost would improve their tilth for seeding the new crops. In winter he repaired implements, cut and hauled wood, and fixed fences, so that no minor jobs would interrupt during the imperative planting season.

No precise day could ever be marked in advance on the kitchen calendar as the date on which the new farm year was to begin. We spoke of March 1 as the calendar's first day of spring, and three weeks later mentioned the vernal equinox. In his diary for 1904 Father made these entries:

> March 1. Came in like a lamb.
> March 2. The lion is commencing to growl.
> March 3. More lamblike, but it is March.

The farm spring really began on the late February morning when Father returned to the house after the barn chores were done and headed for the storeroom.

Over the kitchen, this had been planned as an extra bedroom. It had found better use as a safe and dry place in which to keep the flour supply, the sugar barrel, the seed corn, and whatever else required dry storage. The seed-corn ears, carefully selected at husking time— bright, uniform, well-filled ears with straight rows— rested on a wooden rack against the south wall. Father cut small squares from a cardboard shoe box and numbered them. With the tip of his knife blade he lifted from each ear three grains, one from near the butt, one from near the tip, and one from the middle, rotating the ear so that no two grains came from the same or adjoining rows. Crisscrossed string marked into squares the flat testing box that had been partly filled with earth and covered with muslin. The three grains were laid in a numbered location, and the correspondingly numbered bit of cardboard was attached to the ear by an eight-penny nail punched into the pith of the cob, and the ear returned to the rack. The seeds were covered with dampened muslin and the box set by the window.

After a few days he examined the results. Most of the grains could be expected to be sprouting vigorously. Weak ones would have sprouted slowly, and sometimes others would have shown no signs of life. Thus detected in advance, the sterile and weaker ears were laid aside. One bad ear, Father said, could result in nearly a thousand fewer stalks in the field and in ten or twelve fewer bushels at harvest.

"This is just about the most profitable work on the farm," he often remarked.

When the testing was finished, he shelled and discarded the irregularly shaped grains from the tips and

58

butts of the good ears. The planter, he pointed out, did its work more accurately when the seed grains were uniform in size and shape. Usually he shelled the seed ears by hand to avoid injuring the grains by the mechanical sheller's rough treatment. More snow might fall and more freezes come, but the first essential of spring work had been done. The seed corn was ready.

When hybrid corn became universal, the seed-testing routine was to disappear from the individual farms; but that was in the then unforeseen future. The hybrid seed, now carefully produced by specialized growers, adds many bushels to an acre's yield and has other merits. It is tested, graded, and ready for the planter when sold. But in Father's time the scientists were still trying to find whether their genetic curiosities might have a practical value.

Snow might still be on the ground, but spring was in the air when Father appeared with a handful of elder stems from Gordon's little swamp down the road. With his always sharp jackknife he cut them into one-foot lengths, removed the bark, and took a horizontal slice off one end of each so that, after he had punched out the pith with a heavy wire, each became half tube and half trough. Four sugar maples stood in the pasture—tall, healthy trees that had escaped becoming lumber because they had something better to give. With brace and bit he bored a shallow hole into each about two feet aboveground, and then fitted one of the elder spiles into the hole. A clean pail was set on blocks underneath, and in a few minutes the sweet-tasting sap began to drip from the ends of the spiles. By next morning we might find the pail nearly full. Mother boiled the sap on the kitchen stove—there was too little for a real "sugar bush" operation—until we had several quarts to pour on the morning pancakes.

The supply was never enough for a whole year. "Bring me some nice, clean corn cobs," Mother was pretty sure to say before the maple syrup was quite all used up. I saw the cobs go into her kettle, along with some brown sugar, and remember well enough that the product that emerged was practically indistinguishable from the genuine maple syrup. Not until years afterward did I learn that xylose, the kind of sugar in corn cobs, resembles that in the maple tree.

The *Farm Journal* food editors heard about the corn cob syrup with such polite skepticism that I challenged them to try an experiment in the office kitchens. The result was so satisfactory that they published the recipe, and this was it: "Break two dozen red corn cobs in pieces; cover with boiling water to keep cobs covered; remove cobs, strain, boil down to half; add sugar cup for cup to liquid; boil to consistency desired. Pinch of cream of tartar will prevent crystallizing."

As the days grew longer and more intervals of mild weather appeared, Father could be seen scanning the morning and evening indications with particular attention. On the first windless morning, as soon as the spring breezes had dried the surface fairly well, he would hasten to the wheat field at daybreak without his breakfast. On his shoulder, or maybe in a wheelbarrow, he would carry a bushel of red clover seed. This valuable commodity cost five or even twelve dollars a bushel, and no single grain dared be wasted. It had to be stored in a new canvas bag, and care taken that no gnawing mouse opened a hole. At the field he took a two-quart tin measure and transferred some seed into the "fiddle." This wood, canvas, and tin affair was devised to hang comfortably over the shoulder and to hold a supply of seed, which could dribble out through an adjustable slot onto a star-shaped tin wheel. Once the slot was opened, Father started briskly across the field. His right arm steadily worked the fiddle bow back and forth to spin the wheel, which scattered the seed evenly for eight to ten feet on either side. In a few hours a good many acres could be seeded. If the wind rose strongly enough to deflect the seed, he would stop and wait for another quiet morning.

After a mild winter the wheat by this time might already be showing a measure of new green spring vigor. If the cold had been severe and continuous, it looked gray and pale, but it responded quickly once the sun stimulated the pulsing chlorophyll. When the wheat had been drilled, late the previous September, timothy seed had been sown simultaneously. The drill had a compartment and mechanism for grass seeds. By the time the wheat was ready to harvest around July 1, the ground was well covered with small plants of both red clover and timothy. After the taller wheat was removed, they grew vigorously under the direct sun. By the time another June arrived, the field was rich with clover mixed with a little timothy. When that hay crop had been stored in the barn, the clover again grew up quickly and could be expected to produce a seed crop in the fall. By the next year, unless the sod had been plowed under, the clover, a biennial plant, had disappeared and the field grew only timothy. Except for horses, timothy was not highly regarded as feed, and we seldom let it grow by itself.

The rotation of crops in those years was an established and widely accepted principle that all good farmers followed. Father's basic rotation plan called for wheat or oats one year, clover the second, and corn the third. This could be varied a little, as by letting a field produce hay for two years in succession, or by sowing oats one year and following it with wheat. The important points were to grow clover, and not to raise corn for more than one year, or two at most, in the same field.

The clover was esteemed, not only as a superior feed, but as a soil-building crop. A leguminous plant, it extracted some nitrogen from the air, accumulated it on root nodules, and left it in the ground. Although Father's figures did not attempt to estimate exactly the value of each crop, it is probable that neither the oats nor hay, and maybe not the wheat, paid much profit. Wheat, one of the few crops not wholly consumed on the farm, was sold for cash. Actually, however, the small grains, wheat or oats, were grown primarily to ensure a clover stand, and the clover was grown mainly to help fertilize the corn; and the corn, when fed to animals, produced most of the farm's profits.

The rotation principle has lost much of its importance today, when improved and economical commercial plant foods permit growing corn or other preferred crops year after year in the same fields. In some situations, however, a change of crops is desirable to prevent multiplication of pests or of undesirable soil organisms.

Another preliminary early spring job was to grease the harness. A warmish, sunny day would see the big barn doors pushed wide open. All the harness was brought out and hung on low racks. Every strap and piece was removed, thoroughly cleaned, then rubbed with harness oil until all the leather was black and shiny. This was supposed to make the harness more durable; for a week or so it became less pleasant to handle. If there was any brass, that, too, was polished, but Father never bought harness for show. He regarded brass trimmings as useless ornaments that would require unproductive work.

Sheepshearing came a little later before the spring work really opened up. Father always hired a professional to do this work. For many years he paid Billy Burns, a jovial little Englishman, eight cents a sheep for shearing; later a pleasant, dignified gentleman named William Haines carried on. Father would bring them out from their homes in Ada, and they boarded with us until shearing was finished.

The sheep were penned inside, close to the barn's big sliding doors, and the driveway was swept clean. Near the open doors, where the light was best, a small platform ten or twelve feet square was prepared with clean, smooth boards. The large steel shears were sharpened, shears with wide blades that came to points but were not crossed like scissors; the metal was all in one piece and so designed that the lower part worked as a spring to open the blades the instant the cutting pressure ceased. (Now electric clippers are used.)

A sheep was caught by a hind leg and brought to the platform. Mr. Burns knew exactly how to throw her off her feet and turn her so that she was seated between his knees, with her head against his shoulders and her four feet pointing outward. The animal accepted this unaccustomed indignity with a short struggle and a plaintive "Ba-a-a!" and then resigned herself to whatever might follow. Starting at the point of her breastbone, the shears rapidly parted the wool from the skin. Deftly turning the sheep as he progressed, in fifteen or twenty minutes Mr. Burns would have detached the fleece, snipped off the short trimmings from her head, knees, and tail, and instead of a gray sheep we had a yellowish-white one. She was released, invariably bleating lusty "Ba-a-a's" as she hurried to re-join her friends in what looked as the day progressed more and more like an ovine nudist colony.

The fleece was then carefully spread out. The short trimmings were placed in the middle, and the whole rolled and folded into a squarish bundle that was tied tightly with a heavy jute cord. Woolen mills objected to fleeces tied with sisal binder twine; the fibers were hard to separate from the wool. In later years paper twine took the place of jute. Once bundled, the fleeces were stored in a clean grain bin, or in some out-of-the-way upstairs corner where a canvas cover could protect them from dust and trash.

The wool was not sold until Father thought that the market was good. At times he held it over for a better year. Wool was one commodity that did not deteriorate. The wool buyer brought huge burlap bags, many times the size of our familiar two-bushel grain sacks. A bag was suspended on a frame so that its bottom could not touch the floor, and the fleeces tossed into it. Shortly the buyer or Father would lower himself into the bag to trample the fleeces into the tightest possible space. A boy thought it quite remarkable to see a man completely disappear into a bag. When filled the bag's top was firmly sewn by a huge needle and twine.

Then, to find how much it weighed! The steelyards, to Father an indispensable farm tool, were brought out. They would weigh quite accurately anything two men could lift. A steel bar, notched to the single pound, sustained a sliding, pear-shaped iron balance. A rope sling was slipped under the bag, live calf, sheep, or whatever was to be weighed. The sling was attached to a large hook that dangled from one end of the steel bar. Then, after a fork handle or similar sturdy stick was thrust under a smaller hook attached above the bar's end, two men shouldered the ends of the stick and lifted. The balance was moved until the weight was determined. If the weight was considerable, it was a real relief when the bar balanced out horizontally and the load could be dropped.

The hour that finally and definitively marked the beginning of a new farm year came when the first furrow was plowed. From then on until early winter, after all the corn had been heaped into the cribs, one could expect only occasional respites from work. Most of those came because weather interrupted. There were times when a boy hoped for bad weather.

The annual plowing of the land—lifting and turning the soil for planting crops around the world each year—consumes more power than any other task man undertakes. In these days, when hulking, high-speed tractors roar across the fields making the earth fly behind multibottomed plows, most farmers have forgotten, and many have never even seen, the plodding pre–World War I plowman. Day after day he walked, guiding the plow behind a straining two-horse team, to turn one furrow at a time. But the job was one of primary importance, and men took pride in doing it well.

One did not just suddenly decide to hitch to the plow and begin turning the earth for a new crop. The time had to have come. For several days Father would have gone out to examine the texture of the soil and to determine when it was reasonably dry. Weeks before, he had taken the plow points to the blacksmith to be sharpened and had made certain that no clevises, doubletrees or other essentials were missing or out of order.

Still in February in some years, and seldom later than early March, the plowman would hitch Ben and Nora to the plow and go to the driest corner of the field. He let the plow drag on its side until the spot was chosen at which to set the point into the first furrow. Further preliminaries tested his skill and experience. He had to decide upon the size of the first "land." Depending upon its dimensions, the field would be plowed in several "lands," each at least a hundred and maybe two hundred feet broad.

A good idea was to leave the horses stand while you stepped off an appropriate distance from the side fence to the center of the first land. If you had a good measuring eye, or if a distinctive fence post stood there, you might be able to estimate the equidistant location at the other end of the field. It was better, though, to put up a stake for a marker, tie your handkerchief to its top, and drive empty to the opposite end. Then, if you again stepped off an equal distance from the fence, you were less likely to have to plow a number of short furrows to square up the land, and your last furrow would come out exactly parallel to the fence as it should.

Having determined the starting point, you tied the lines together behind your back and lifted the plow handles slightly so that the point would plunge into the ground. You fixed your eyes between the horses upon the handkerchief marker at the other end. You shouted, "Git up!" The horses, fresh and willing, seemed to sense the importance of the moment and wanted to pull too fast. The plow bit into the ground, too deeply at first. You pressed the handles down slightly and leveled it off at four or five inches—the first furrow should be shallow—held hard to keep the handles steady, kept a close eye on your marker, cried "Gee!" and "Haw!" or pulled on the right or left lines, and hoped to find a perfectly straight furrow behind you when you pushed the plow handles down to emerge at the marker.

When you looked back, you wondered why the furrow was a little wavery, not quite as straight as you had hoped it would be. The next furrow was an equally difficult though less tense task. The "near" horse, the left member of the team, naturally tried to avoid walking on the soft, freshly turned earth. He preferred solid sod for his footing. He was likely to go first on one and then on the other side of the new furrow. This did not matter too much, though, because the line had been drawn and minor mistakes could be corrected.

Once a land was started, the plowing was mostly a matter of walking between the handles and keeping the plow at the right depth. One horse walked in the furrow and the other on the unplowed ground. They required little guidance. It was easy unless the plow failed to "scour." That was exasperating. A small spot of rust, no bigger than a quarter, could prevent the earth from sliding smoothly off the curved steel moldboard. Shortly a growing lump adhered to the spot until the plow could not lift and turn the soil as it should. The plowman had no choice then except to turn the plow on its side, scrape off the sticky earth, and try to grind off the rusty spot. In gritty soil friction with gravelly particles might be expected to shine up the moldboard, but loamy soil had no scouring power. The sensible course then was to get a bucket of water and a brick, and rub until the rust disappeared. Father nearly always made sure that when the plows were put away after use they received a thick coating of grease to prevent any speck of rust from making trouble next season.

Since the horses had the hard work to do, and would be as busy as the men all summer, simple wisdom demanded that they be treated considerately. During the first week or so of plowing days they were permitted to stop for frequent rests, because their muscles were soft from the comparative idleness of winter. On warm days, when their breathing became fast, the plow was stopped to allow them to cool off. Occasionally one went forward to lift their collars to see that no shoulder sores were developing, and to scrape off the loose hairs and perspiration that could cause smooth leather to rub. A sore shoulder that first week of plowing might mean a horse partially disabled soon afterward, maybe for all summer. That denoted careless management.

A boy could plow as well as a man as soon as he grew tall enough to grip the handles firmly. He liked the job. He felt that he had become the equal of a man. He could enjoy holding and guiding the plow, directing the team, looking back occasionally to see whether his furrow was straighter than the previous one, and smelling the fresh earth as it turned up to the service of the season. When the horses needed a pause, he could ease his legs, either by sitting on the plow beam or by leaning upon the crosspiece between the handles. There, for a few idle moments, he could watch the bronzed grackles, their rainbow spring plumage glistening as they explored the new furrow for grackle delicacies. He could listen to the gay "cheerio" of the meadowlarks, try to glimpse the black crescent marks in their brilliant yellow breast plumage, and speculate as to which tuft of grass along the fence they might be selecting for a nest. Now and then a flight of wild ducks might be seen hurrying north, and more rarely the stately V's of migrating Canada geese. Killdeers called their names and skittered boldly nearby. Horned larks in little flocks and vesper sparrows singly or in pairs ran along fearlessly. Before the plowing would be finished, he could expect bobolinks to entertain him from the adjacent hayfields, dickcissels from the fence wires, and to see the handsome redheaded woodpeckers decorating the posts. Spring plowing was pleasant, especially when the plowboy knew he must often let the horses rest.

Even though the weather turned overcoat-cold and the top half-inch of soil had frozen, plowing could continue; but not when the ground was very wet. Our soil was a clay loam of a type that, if plowed when too wet, dried into rock-hard clods. Though suspended after heavy rains, plowing went on intermittently until all the corn ground was turned over.

An interruption came in late March or early April in order to sow the oats. Oats were always seeded in a field that had borne corn the year before. Old-timers plowed their oats ground, but later farmers had found that the crop yielded as well and tended to stand up better without plowing. The disk was used instead. This simple machine had two series of sharp, concave steel disks fastened at intervals on a shaft. With levers one could change the angle and depth of cut. If the blades ran straight forward they cut lightly; if at a sharper angle, they stirred the ground three or four inches deep. The disk quickly reduced the topsoil and trash to a shallow seedbed. The two-horse drill accomplished the sowing. A special compartment in the drill permitted grass seeds to be sown at the same time. Oats, however, were not regarded as the best "nurse crop" for grasses. They shaded the plants more heavily than wheat; and the weaker straws too often broke down and lodged before harvest, so as to kill out the new undergrowth of grass or clover.

Modern grain drills also include mechanisms for distributing commercial fertilizer while the grain is being sown. After his first experiment with acid phosphate as a crop stimulant, about 1912, Father bought a new drill for that purpose. He never thereafter sowed wheat without adding the fertilizer.

Father always aimed to finish planting the corn by May 10. Weather sometimes delayed him, but after that date he thought it began to be too late. Data from the Ohio Experiment Station later confirmed this observation; it said that for every day's delay after May 10 one less bushel per acre could be expected. The date also conformed to the ancient signs observed by Indians and early settlers, who planted their corn when the white oaks' leaves were as large as squirrel's ears, or by the day when the redheaded woodpeckers arrived.

Around May 1, then, the spike-toothed harrow began to smooth the plowed fields. To this framework of iron pipes heavy iron teeth, each six or eight inches long, were bolted. The slant of the teeth could be adjusted by a lever. The harrow leveled off the rough surface and helped to break up the clods. The first time over we harrowed double, with an overlap, and then went crosswise. Three or four harrowings normally were necessary. Walking all day over the loose earth was more tiresome, more hurried, and less exciting than plowing. After a rain, though, one bit of interest was to scan the little pebbles and stones that had been exposed. Any sizable stone was carried off and tossed by a fence post. One never knew when he might find an Indian relic—an arrowhead, a hammer, a stone ax, or even, as I once did find, a stone pestle. We always saved these artifacts our predecessors had left behind.

The object of all this preparation, of course, was to create a suitable seedbed for the corn. After the harrowing we used a drag, a simple device of thick planks with edges overlapped and firmly nailed. This would smooth the surface and crumble small clods into dust. Father wanted the top two inches to be so fine that each planted grain would be in full contact with soil and no empty interstices left underneath.

A hired man or a boy could plow, harrow, and drag. The corn planter, however, demanded the highest possible skill. Father always took the best team and drove the planter himself.

In his earlier years he drilled the corn; that is,

single seeds were dropped at intervals ten or twelve inches apart. Later he adopted the checkrow system, by which the planter dropped three or four grains in each hill in such a manner that the rows ran geometrically both ways across the field. This made it possible to drive the cultivators both ways and to reach nearly all the weeds. Farmers argued as to which method was best; but when labor became too expensive for hoeing, the checkrow plan came to be preferred.

The simple device that accomplished the checkrow's uniformity often mystified people who had not seen it used. On one occasion a noted scientist, who had frequently flown across the corn country, asked me how farmers could place their corn in such regular geometric patterns. I explained that the corn was usually planted in hills 40 or 42 inches apart. A wire was unrolled across the field. At corresponding intervals the wire had a small knot that, as it passed through a small V-shaped device at the side of the planter, tripped the seed plate and dropped the grains. Metal stakes at each end of the field held the wire taut, and after each crossing the stakes had to be moved to a new position. If the wire was always kept at the same tension, the crossrows would be just as regular and straight as the long rows.

My scientist friend understood the explanation, but was appalled at the idea of the driver having to get off the planter so often to move the wire. Seizing a pencil and pad, he set out to design a better method. He had no more success than several million farmers had had, even though they, too, had thought that a less laborious scheme would be desirable.

Hybrid seed, modern fertilizers, power machines,

and constant research have brought important new ideas into the cornfields. Rows only thirty, or even twenty-two, inches apart are now not uncommon. Instead of the weeks spent in plowing, harrowing, and smoothing the soil, machines now make it possible to plow and plant in a single operation. The number of plants per acre has been doubled, from eight or ten thousand to fifteen or even more than twenty thousand.

The ability of hybrid strains to utilize plant food ingredients, and the ability of superior fertilizers to supply these ingredients, have boosted the national average yields of even thirty years ago from about twenty-five to more than eighty bushels per acre, and in at least two instances yields of three hundred bushels have been achieved. If the boy of 1910 were to return to the same farm with the same methods, he would be hopelessly outclassed by his least efficient neighbor.

After the last corn row was planted, the pressure to hurry lessened for a few days. Now was the time for another project that was among the most welcome of the whole year. This was the annual fishing trip.

The previous day Father greased the buggy axles, dug an ample supply of angleworms, and in the evening checked over the hooks, lines, and sinkers. Mother prepared an advance supply of food. Soon after sunrise the next morning we started in gay humor on the eighteen-mile drive. The route took us south through McGuffey and into the Scioto marsh, where for several miles we could note the groups of workers on their knees as they weeded the onion crop. After crossing the narrow Scioto River we reached high ground again, then drove through Roundhead, the oldest village in the county and the only one with no railroad. Near the Logan

County line we could sniff the waters of the reservoir, one arm of which came into view before we reached Newland's Landing, or Turkey Foot.

This was the Lewiston Reservoir, known now as Indian Lake. When the Miami and Erie Canal had been dug, back in the 1840s, the reservoir had been dammed up to feed the canal. About five miles long and four wide, it was then Ohio's second largest body of water.

At Newland's Landing Father and three neighbors had built a small cabin for overnight shelter on fishing and hunting trips. They called it a shanty; "cabin" and "cottage" were names too pretentious to suit them. Four bunks were nailed against the walls. Mother laughed for years over my earliest report about a stay at the reservoir because I said I had slept in a "trough." The bunks did look a little like the feed troughs we had in the barn. The furniture included a long table, an old cook stove, and a few benches and chairs.

Upon arrival at the shanty Old Doc was hurriedly unhitched and taken to the barn provided by the landing's owner. The food was carried inside, and a rowboat was hired. The boat cost twenty-five cents a day; that, and some horse feed, were usually the only cash outlay. Long cane poles were kept stored in the shanty. Within half an hour the three of us could be pushing off.

Father was a good oarsman and had a sharp eye for likely fishing places. Corks—ordinary corks saved from large bottles—were adjusted for floats, hooks baited, and then it was a quiet race to see who could catch the first fish. By late afternoon we had a plentiful string of bluegills, sunfish, perch, and bullheads. Usually a neighbor family made the trip at the same time. The men cleaned fish, and supper was a picnic fish fry. The taste of fish was thoroughly savored. As anyone knows who has fried them fresh from cool waters, the delicate flavors of these panfish species are superb. To us, who seldom had other fish during the year, they were a rare delight.

Next morning, soon after dawn, we would be out for more fishing. By mid-afternoon we had to start home. One was never quite ready for that moment, but it had to come. We drove back over the eighteen-mile, four-hour trip, happy to have had the privileges and fun we had enjoyed.

This was the end of spring. The memories added cheer to the more arduous toils that the longer days of summer were about to introduce.

Chapter 6

The Lively Old Summertime

The yield of corn could, before summer's end, be hurt by weather, weeds, insects, some mysterious disease, or an unrecognized deficiency in the soil. No one could control the weather.

A good "stand," though, could be assured by taking pains to see that every space had a seed and that every seed sent up a stalk. A few days after planting, Father went out to squat by the rows and with fingers to uncover a few of the seed grains. A glance could reveal whether they were germinating normally. Bad seed, if any had been planted, did not grow. Failure could follow where seeds fell in a poorly prepared spot so that they lay among clods where no moisture stimulated the germs to sprout. In a poorly drained location, seed might rot rather than germinate after a heavy rain.

Father was pretty sure to load the "jabber"—a hand-operated planter—with leftover seed corn and re-plant in every spot where stalks were missing. A special danger was from cutworms, most likely to appear in fields where sod had been plowed under. These brown, smooth worms, an inch or more long, could go down a row and cut off, just under the surface, a dozen young corn plants in succession.

As soon as the young corn had unfolded two or three leaves, it was time to go over whole field again with the spiketooth harrow. The teeth, slanted to stir only the top inch of soil, did no harm to the corn. They did turn up millions of tiny weed and grass sprouts that the sun would wither and kill. This was the most important cultivation of the season.

The first morning after school was out in spring, Father had a question ready for me. "Which team do you want to handle this summer, son?" He knew what answer to expect. It was always "I'll take the mules."

Before breakfast every workday one first hurried to the barn to feed the work stock. They needed plenty of time to eat before going to the fields. Then they were curried and brushed and harnessed. The mules, coarser-haired than horses, were much easier to keep clean. Moreover, they were smaller, and their harness was easier to put on. Marve Phillips was not far wrong when he said that I liked the mules because I could throw the brush at one, the currycomb at the other, put on the harness, and be ready for breakfast.

Father had paid $206 for Jack and Joe, the two mules, in 1904. Both were gentle, well trained, and easy to handle.

By the time the mules and I had harrowed the corn, it was high enough to start the cultivators. Swinging gangs of three shovels each were suspended on springs under a framework between two high steel wheels. A seat was so located that the rider bestrode and looked down upon the corn row. By holding a foot in a stirrup, he controlled with leg power the sidewise movement of each gang of shovels. The effort required was not much, but the sidewise swing called into play a set of little-used thigh muscles that for the first few days were sure to complain.

Old-timers, who insisted that only by walking could one do a really precise job, considered the riding cultivator to be a lazy man's tool. Our neighbor, Joe Powell, followed his walking cultivator to the end of his eighty years, long after anyone else adhered to the old way. He was charged, no doubt falsely, with having remarked, "If the Lord had intended cultivators to have seats, He would have made 'em that way."

The first cultivation went slowly. One carried a lath about three feet long, one end whittled to a paddle shape. He kept his eyes on the small corn plants as they passed under him; if the shovels covered one with soil, he stopped the team and reached back with the stick to free its leaves.

"Plowing corn," as everyone except my father called the process—he always called it "cultivating"—was pleasant work. Although it required closer attention than regular plowing, it came at the most delightful of seasons, late May and through June. One worked at it alone with his team and could dream about tomorrows without neglecting the duties of the day.

The second and third cultivations were easier than the first because by then the corn had grown high enough that no halts were needed to uncover stalks. One drove steadily along to the end of the field and back again. The team knew where to walk. One guided the shovels, regulated their depth, hoped to exterminate all the weeds, and kept the surface stirred on the theory that loose soil interrupted the processes of capillary attraction and kept undergound the moisture that growing corn demanded in large quantities. The second cultivation, if the corn had been planted in checkrows, was crosswise. This was not so easy if the planter wire had not been kept uniformly taut, and no excuse was acceptable for plowing out a hill or cutting the roots too closely. Before the third cultivation had been finished, the tops of the stalks would be bending under the cultivator frame. "Knee-high by the Fourth of July" was usually achieved.

Only a slack farmer failed to cultivate his corn at least three times. Four times was not regarded as too many, but hay and wheat harvest came too soon most years to permit the fourth plowing.

Before the third cultivation was finished, Father had noticed that a third of the blossoms in the clover field had begun to turn brown. The rapid clickety-clack of the mowing machine soon thereafter proclaimed that hay time had arrived.

On the second morning after the mowing started, Father announced that we probably could not cultivate all day. Hay should be dry enough to put into the barn. Thereafter, if our third cultivation was not complete, we had to try to get it done in the mornings before the dew dried from the hay.

No great enthusiasm hailed the hay harvest. It was a job that had to be done, and we expected to get it done, even though some of the work was sure to be hot, hard, and unpleasant. We knew that when it was over we would all be glad and could share in a sense of achievement for having helped to get it done.

Haymaking brought into use a wholly different set of equipment. The mowing, of course, came first.

Father planned to mow each day only as much as could likely be brought into the barn two days later. On the second day, and perhaps again on the morning of the third day, the tedder went to work. This wheeled device had a series of pitchfork-like prongs so mounted that, as the horses pulled it forward, the forks tossed the mown hay into the air and let it fall lightly for the sun and the circulating air to dry. If enough moisture had been evaporated, along late in the third morning the rake was brought out. One horse pulled the rake. That job usually fell to Old Doc, the driving horse, and he resented the imposition. Doc felt that he was a road horse and never was cheerful about being hitched to any field instrument. The rake drew the scattered hay into windrows.

The hay wagon carried a wide rack. The bottom "sling"—an arrangement of ropes and four stout wooden bars—was spread over the rack. In the field, one man stood on the wagon to place the hay so that the load was evenly distributed and properly built. He could load for two pitchers. The pitchers walked to the middle of a windrow and lifted the hay aside to make room for the wagon to pass through. The team was stopped so that the windrow was at the wagon's middle. Then, a pitcher on each side gathered a batch of hay with his long-handled, three-tined fork and lifted it onto the rack. This went on until one-fourth of the load was on the wagon, when a second sling was spread, and so on until four slings had been laid and the load was as high as the pitchers could reach or as heavy as the team could easily pull. Then the loader drove to the barn while the pitchers walked briskly behind.

The load was drawn through the big double doors

and halted at the exact center of the barn. Someone quickly unhitched the horses from the wagon and brought them around to the barn front where they were hitched to the end of a long, stout rope. The man on the load caught up the two ends of the sling and fastened them to a special pulley suspended over his head. He saw that his trip rope was snapped to its mate dangling under the sling. The team was started. The rope moved through an arrangement of pulleys that first lifted the top slingload straight overhead to the center of the roof, where its pulley latched into a "car" that then slid along a steel track to whichever end of the barn was being filled. A stout pull on the trip rope parted the sling at the bottom, and the load fell. While the team returned to the barn doors, the man on the wagon pulled back his empty sling, prepared the second slingload, and the field pitchers, now in the mow, spread out the hay, pushing forkloads into the farthest corners to make sure that it was well spread and no space wasted. This went on until the wagon was emptied. Then everyone took a drink of cold water and hurried to the field for another load. Four loads made a good afternoon's stint.

Later Father decided that one sling to clean off the bottom of the load was a good idea, but four took too much time to accomplish a result that a simpler method could achieve. Thereafter, two double harpoon forks were used to take off all except the bottom part of the load, and with two trip ropes they worked very well. He also bought a hayloader, which, hitched behind the wagon, elevated hay from the swath, eliminated raking and pitching, and saved some time. The hayloader did not greatly reduce the muscular effort. Two men had to ride the wagon to move the hay forward to build a good load, and it helped if also a boy was handy to drive the team.

As hay piled up in the mows and came closer to the roof, and as it became riper and drier and dustier, the men in the mow found their work hotter, harder, and dirtier. Our barn had a metal roof, which on a perfect haymaking day in no way diminished the thermal effect of the sun. After every load all hands drank liberally from a gallon earthen jug freshly filled with cool water. On especially hot days Mother brought out cold water spiced with vinegar and ginger; or if ice was on hand, she made lemonade.

For years I kept on the wall of my offices an enlarged photograph of our barn. When tempted to complain of the heat while sitting at a desk with an electric fan or air-conditioner going, I looked at that old galvanized roof and remembered how it felt while struggling to push a mass of tangled hay back under the rafters in mid-afternoon when the humidity was high and the thermometer stood around 90 degress.

Before hay harvest ended, the corn had outgrown the cultivators. One rainy morning we took off the shovels, sharpened them, covered them with axle grease, and laid them up for another year.

No sooner had the last of the hay been stowed away than time had come to cut wheat. The binder cut the standing grain and tied it into bundles with sisal twine. The bundles were dropped on a carrier until six or seven had accumulated. Then the driver pushed a foot lever that let them fall in windrows.

The next job was shocking up the bundles, and that was hard work—next to corn-cutting the most tiresome of the year. Two men usually teamed together, although a lone worker could manage. One picked up two bundles and set them firmly, butt ends down, against two bundles similarly placed by the other man. Around the four bundles six others were added so that ten in all were standing together, all leaning a trifle toward the center. Each man picked up one bundle more, put his left arm under its center, and held the butts against his stomach while he parted and spread the heads of the straw. These two bundles, the "cap sheaves," were placed carefully on top to shelter the others from rain. The result was called a "shock" of grain. If properly set up, a shock could stand for weeks, undamaged by rain or wind.

Bending to pick up thousands of sheaves one after another and grabbing into the straw with bare hands were hard on both back and hands. One's fingers sometimes grew raw, and one's back felt even worse. Those of the Golden Years were born "thirty years too soon" to have enjoyed the swift ease of the combine-harvesters that now cut and thresh the grain during one pass.

Shortly after the wheat harvest came the oats. This was a little less arduous because the bundles were not so heavy nor the straw so stiff. Picking them up and setting them on end all day, however, was not a highly amusing form of entertainment.

If a small boy was around, not big enough to help shock the grain, he always managed to be in the field at the finish of cutting. Rabbits, seeking to escape from the clattering binder, would keep moving deeper into the standing grain. They did not know that soon no hiding place would be left. Sometimes, as this knowledge dawned, and a frightened small rabbit dashed confusedly out into the stubble, the boy could run down and catch him. Wild rabbits did not, as he hoped, readily become pets. He learned that after caging one or two victims, which refused to eat and soon died. Thereafter, though it might be fun to try to catch one, it was released soon after the capture.

The older farmers all knew how to tie a bundle of grain with its own straw. When men cut the grainfields with the sickle or cradle, and before the automatic tying device came to the binder, no one thought of buying twine to tie the bundles. The cash outlay would have seemed extravagant. With a little practice one could pick up a handful of loose straw, grasp it firmly with the left hand just below the heads, divide it into equal parts, make a twist around the heads, wrap the two parts around the bundle and with a quick twist and push leave the sheaf as tightly fastened as a binder could do with twine. Since the binder occasionally missed tying a bundle, the old art was still useful to those who followed it to do the shocking.

The accelerated tempo that was felt from the start of plowing until the corn was planted, and from the beginning of hay harvest until the oats were shocked, slackened off again at that point. Plenty of work waited to be done before September, when the corn harvest would begin, but for five or six weeks the pressure was a little less and not so constant. Still, some sizable jobs remained to be done, all of them important.

Most interesting of these was the threshing.

Chapter 7

Threshing—the Glamor Job

For at least three decades the way we threshed our grain has been superseded by swifter, more economical machines and methods. Yet, from Pennsylvania to California, late in each summer, old-fashioned steam traction engines and grain separators are assembled and the out-dated process repeated. In few of the annual agricultural play days are other of the old-time work jobs reenacted, unless at an occasional plowing match the two-horse plow appears as a sideshow. Threshing must have been even more glamorous than it seemed back in those years when it was spelled the same but always pronounced *thrashing*.

Threshing required a dozen to twenty hands and was therefore a neighborhood cooperative project. Farmers "changed work" with each other, each furnishing a team and wagon and one or more men.

The threshing rig was owned by a specialist. His heavy steam engine, which could move along the road at two or three miles an hour, hauled the separator. A team of horses pulled the water tank behind it. The machine crew included the engineer, who was usually the owner, two separator hands, and the water-hauler.

Wood or coal for the engine was brought up in advance by the farmer whose grain was about to be threshed.

When our turn came, we watched to see the outfit steaming slowly up our road. Gates were opened, and someone made sure that all the livestock was properly confined. Jugs were filled with cold water. The engine chugged through the lane and on out behind the barn. Father indicated where he wanted the "set" to be made in order to place the strawstack in the right location. The separator was maneuvered to the chosen spot, and the engine then turned and lined up, facing it from twenty to thirty feet away. By this time the neighbors' wagons began to arrive, and more or less without direction the drivers would move to the farthest corner of the wheatfield to begin loading bundles.

The wagons were equipped with the same kind of wide racks that were used for bringing in hay, but loading them with grain bundles was a different and slightly more difficult art. The pitcher stabbed a cap sheaf and laid it near a corner of the wagon rack. The loader placed the first bundles so that the butts protruded six or eight inches beyond the edge of the rack. Managing if possible always to use the wider-spread cap sheaves at the corners, he placed a row of bundles all around the wagon. Unless the straw was exceptionally long, the heads would barely touch in the middle. When the first round was complete, he placed a row down the middle, alternating the butts from left to right so that they reached about to the twine bands of the outer row. The pitcher, if he were expert and cooperative, managed to lay each bundle "right end to" at the exact spot where the loader could pick it up quickly with the least effort. Another round was added

88

and then another, until the load reached so high in the air that the pitcher had to begin to toss the bundles off the end of his fork. If the loader had done his work well, he could drive up to the separator with his load intact, no matter how rough the field. If not, a whole corner of the load might slide to the ground. This meant not only the delay of reloading, but loud and merry derision from all hands. Consequently, most farmers learned to be skilled bundle-loaders.

By the time the first load came in, the separator had been chunked and staked firmly so that the pull of the belt would not move it from position. The engineer moved the engine to see that its flywheel and the beltwheel of the separator were exactly in line. The long, leather belt had been unrolled, crossed in the middle, and hung on the flywheels. The engine was backed a few inches to give the belt proper tension.

The engineer gave the whistle a little toot and slowly started the belt to moving. If the alignment was faulty, the belt would fall off. Only a rare thresherman found no cusswords to use while the condition was hastily corrected. That done, the separator began to rattle and soon to whir. As soon as the engineer satisfied himself that all was in order, another toot directed the men on the loads to begin tossing their bundles into the self-feeder. Shortly the straw began to emerge from the blower, a long ten-inch pipe at the rear through which a large fan blew the threshed straw out onto the stack. In a moment the weigher would click and the first half-bushel of the new harvest would be tripped into the sack fastened at the lower end of the dump pipe. Father was quick to reach for a handful to examine the plumpness and quality of the grain and to see how cleanly the machine was threshing. Before long he would be seen holding his hand out some distance in the blower stream to detect whether any of the wheat was being blown out with the straw, a fault some threshermen committed through improper adjustments of the separator machinery, although since they were paid by the bushel it was to their advantage to get all the grain possible into the sacks.

The choicest jobs at threshing time were either to be a field pitcher or to attend to the grain-sacking. Field pitching was cleaner and not too arduous because wagons seldom came fast enough to keep the pitchers busy continuously. Hauling threshed grain from the machine to the storage bins was not too hard on some farms, but a strenuous job on others where bags had to be lifted to some high overhead bin. Few Ohio farmers at that time thought of selling wheat direct from threshing. It was stored until some months later when the market usually was better. The dirtiest assignment was the strawstack or, worse yet, a haymow into which straw was being blown. An afternoon behind the blower on a dusty strawstack or in a dustier mow not infrequently brought chills and fever that night. The effects wore away in a day or so, so we never let it concern us. As straw became less important on farms, it became customary to let the blower, with a little guidance from an occasional attendant, do all the stacking.

The man with the waterwagon had to know the locality well. Not every farm could spare enough water from its well to keep the engine supplied. A dry spell at threshing time might compel the water-hauler to drive a mile or more to fill his tank from a pool under a bridge or from some half-abandoned well from which the owner would give him permission to draw.

Two improvements appeared on threshing machines during the Golden Years. The earlier separators had no self-feeders. Bundles were pitched from the wagons, heads toward the machine, to a shelf from which a crew hand armed with a sharp knife seized them, slashed the twine band, and fed the straw into the separator's whirling rollers. Ray Hullibarger, who worked every year with one of the threshing outfits, had lost his forearm in those dangerous rollers. The self-feeder eliminated the need for a man at this station. Endless chains with steel tines kept the bundles moving forward. The straw blower also saved at least one man's time. On the earlier threshing machines a light carrier elevated the straw a little distance to where one or more men had to push it out of the way and build it into a stack. Larger threshing outfits came, too, big enough that two wagons could be unloaded at once.

No thresherman ever seemed to make much money, even though he kept his engine going much of the year by hulling clover, shredding corn, or running a portable sawmill. The investment was high for the number of operating hours.

Threshing from the field did not come into vogue in our area until early in the new century. Before then the bundles were first stacked near the spot where the strawstack was desired to stand. The art of building a stack of sheafed grain by now has probably disappeared. A low frame of fence rails was laid to hold the stack well off the ground. Then the bundles were placed somewhat as in loading a wagon, but much greater skill was essential. From the bottom each round projected outward a few inches beyond the previous one until the stack was eight or ten feet high. Then each round was withdrawn slightly until the top could be capped with a few bundles. An expert knew exactly how to place the bundles, one upon another, so that none could slip. When he had finished, the stack, whether round or long, was built with what appeared to be almost perfect symmetry. A good stack fifteen feet high or more could withstand winds and storms and keep the grain dry for several months. Father knew how to build a stack and occasionally did, but he preferred to engage the more expert services of Joe Powell, Dal Preston, or Jack Bloodworth. Stacking lengthened the threshing season into late autumn.

Threshing time brought neighbors together who had had little time to visit during the busy spring and summer months. It was always an occasion to catch up on all the neighborhood talk and for much gaiety and banter. An ill-humored threshing occasion was unknown. Farmers might be impatient over the delays before the outfit reached them and might scold the thresherman. Each, however, depended on his neighbors for help, so cheerful good humor was the rule. Occasional interruptions from showers or breakdowns, or morning delays while the fields were drying, were not much regretted. Someone was sure to drive a pair of stakes and start pitching horseshoes.

Feeding the threshermen was a major household task. Mother made preparations for days ahead. Someone had to drive to town to buy a supply of meat, which, before refrigeration, might not keep if the outfit failed to arrive when expected. If that threatened, the meat had to be canned or cold-packed and a new supply obtained. However, no one objected to the absence of butcher shop beef as long as there was plenty of ham from last winter's butchering.

A ten-day wet spell delayed threshing one summer. Finally the weather cleared up, and we got started at Lem Runser's. Bill Shroll, a genial, boastful ne'er-do-well, who had somehow acquired credit enough to buy a secondhand steam engine and separator, had been engaged for most of the neighborhood harvest. After a late start one afternoon, we threshed out a few wagonloads. Bill warned all hands to be ready to go next morning the minute the dew was off.

All were there in good time. The sun dried out the field, and we loaded up, wondering that no humming roar came from the barn. Bill was having engine trouble. About eleven o'clock, after much cursing, repairs were completed, and Bill swore that he would keep us all jumping for the rest of the day. Probably we would finish, he said, although everyone knew that the job would take into the next afternoon.

At noon Bill stopped the machine for dinner, again warning all within hearing that he would stand for no full hour of loafing. He trotted to the house, washed hastily, and was first at the table. Bolting his meal, he ran back to the engine and yanked the whistle cord to tell all hands and the countryside that a big afternoon's threshing was going to start just as soon as a few dawdling diners could leave the table and begin tossing bundles. The whistle kept blowing. It blew and blew. Finally the sound faded out and weakly died away. The whistle had stuck and had blown off all the steam in the boiler.

Still cursing but no longer boasting, Bill built up a new head of steam before mid-afternoon. We had a few horseshoe games, and finished the job next day before sundown.

Before all the wheat had been threshed, the oats shocks would be cured and dry. The threshing outfit went on around its circuit to finish up the wheat, taking the oats, too, and then returned to the first farms where the oats had not been ready. Oats threshing was no different except that the coarser, lighter grain flowed much faster from the separator and kept the bag attendants busier; and oats were much easier to handle at the bins. A bushel of wheat weighs sixty pounds, oats only thirty-two. Now and then a farmer gained temporary unpopularity by raising a field of barley. The prickly awns from ripe barley beards penetrated the clothing and scratched the skins of those who had to handle the crop. No one liked to work on a barley threshing job, but to refuse would have been unneighborly.

As quickly as possible after the grain was threshed, one of the fields, usually the one that had grown oats, had to be plowed for sowing wheat. Plowing in August was a less-inspiriting activity than plowing in April. The ground could be extra hard if a dry spell had continued for long. The big bronze, green-headed horse flies were abundant, and, worse, the botflies had come. The botfly did not bite or sting. It sought only to deposit its eggs on the hairs under the horse's chin or on his fetlock. But by some instinct every horse hated and feared the parasitic botfly and would shake his head, stomp his feet, and become almost frenzied when the little bee-like flies undertook to lay their eggs. At rest stops one

94

tried to capture the botfly in his cupped hand; he had to be swift to succeed.

The third major task in the late summer period was not precisely a glamorous job. It was to clear the barn and feedlot from the manure left after the winter feeding. A whole strawstack and acres of cornstalks would have been consumed in bedding the animals. We hauled out many more than a hundred heavy loads each year. With strong-handled, four-tined forks the hard-packed manure was lifted a forkful at a time into the spreader. When the load was rounded, one man drove to the field. The spreader was a wagon with an endless apron for its bottom and a whirling spike-toothed cylinder at the rear. When the gears were engaged with the rear wheels, the fertilizer was scattered evenly over the ground. Before the spreader was perfected, manure was hauled on a wagon or sled. To scatter it properly then had required almost as much hard work as did the loading.

Nowadays a tractor-operated forklift can clear a stable or feedyard with little exertion from human muscle. Utterly unbelievable to a Golden Years farmer, men now question whether manure is really worth the trouble to haul and spread. Many farmers dispose of it in other ways. Commercial plant foods supply crop needs more completely, precisely, and economically.

In the slack time between oats harvest and corn-cutting, a few other minor jobs were looked after. If late rains had renewed weed growth in parts of the cornfields, so that pigweeds, lambs-quarters, and other heavy moisture consumers were numerous, one might be invited to hitch old Nora, the steadiest horse, to an old-fashioned double shovel plow, or to the little five-shoveled one-horse cultivator, and make round trips through the rows for a day or so. By this time the corn was tasseling out over one's head. A wire muzzle was attached over the horse's mouth so she could not bite off the ears, but the driver had no protection from the sharp leaves and falling dust and pollen. No breeze ever seemed to penetrate the heavy rows. The "double-shovel" was a relic of the mid-nineteenth century, when it was the only kind of cultivator the Ohio pioneers knew.

Or, one might get the fencerow mowing assignment. No machine could handle this. Father would hold the scythe blade to the grindstone until the edge was razor-sharp. It was then replaced on the awkward-looking but actually well-designed long, curved handle called a snath. Whetstone in hip pocket, one coursed the fencerows. The actual mowing was not hard. Most of the rows were cleaned every year, so that little except blue grass grew along the fences, and that did not have to be cut. It was expected, however, that every thistle, burdock, milkweed, ironweed, or other unwelcome species would be felled. Along the one or two remaining old-fashioned zigzag rail fences, one had to be deft to get the scythe blade behind every weed. Along the wire fences one had to be careful not to dull the edge by sweeping it behind a wire. One never knew when he might scare up a rabbit, find the nest of a meadowlark, bob white, or ground sparrow, stir up a bumblebee's nest, or even run into a snake. (It would usually be a garter snake, or perhaps a black snake or milk snake; we had no poisonous species.)

It was exhilarating for a boy to stand the scythe up

96

in front of him, blade pointing outward, and, with hand balanced just right, wield the whetstone with expert, quick, long strokes—first on one side and then the other—that made the blade ring out a message to all the neighborhood that a boy was doing a grown-up job. The more certain he was that someone could hear, the more pains he took to sharpen the blade often.

To keep the roadsides neat, Father preferred to take the scythe himself. For years he fought persistently against the sweet clover that kept starting up along the limestone pikes. It was a weed then. Eventually we began sowing sweet clover as a useful forage and soil-building crop. He hated weeds, and seldom walked anywhere over the farm, if his hands were otherwise empty, without taking along a sharp hoe or his spud to demolish any of these enemies he might encounter. The spud was a special piece of armament. A sturdy, sharp blade about three inches wide, short and spadelike was attached to the lower end of a smooth, straight handle five and a half feet long. It was like a spear with a wide point. When one grasped it with both hands and thrust forcibly at the root of thistle or dock, it cut the weed off cleanly just under the surface. For the taller and tougher weeds, such as mullein, burdock, sour dock, thistles, pokeweed, and others, the spud was an ideal weapon, better than the scythe because it severed them below the crowns.

After threshing had removed the shocks from the grainfields, the war on weeds required mowing the stubble. The binder's cutting blade was usually set to clip the grain stems from eight to twelve or fifteen inches above ground. This left that much length of strawy stubble. Weeds as well as clover and timothy began vigorous growth after the grain was cut. Ragweed could spring up and make seed before frost, and ragweed seed, the Experiment Stations had told us, could remain viable in the soil for thirty years. So the mowing machine was kept clattering until all the wheat and oats stubble had been clipped close. The operation restrained the weeds and did not hurt the young grasses. The cut stubble disintegrated and did not appear in next year's hay, as it tended to do when left standing.

For Canada thistles Father reserved his most vigorous hatred and topmost vigilance. Unlike the ordinary thistles, which were conspicuous, easily spudded out, and spread only where the winds floated their downy seeds, the Canada thistle also spread rapidly from underground roots. Once established, it was difficult to eradicate. The Canada thistles could start from an airborne seed blown from the neglected patch of a faraway neighbor. The seed sometimes made its entry by way of hay, feed, or grass seed brought in by purchase. The first tiny plants could start unnoticed in a pasture corner and be firmly established before anyone knew they were there. They might peep up in a cultivated cornfield late in the season. If not restrained, a patch only a yard across could in an astonishingly few years take over an acre and grow so thick that no crop could compete.

When he spotted a start of Canada thistles in the pasture, Father did not depend on his efficient spud or his sharp hoe. He carried a can of kerosene to the scene, with his jackknife cut off below its crown every thistle he could find, and poured kerosene generously on the roots. Two or three weeks later, he went again to administer the same treatment to whatever new thistles had sprung up from roots not destroyed. As long as a bit of root lived it could send up a stem, and one stem could soon foster many thistles. When sheep were in the pasture, he gave them their salt on the spots where thistles had been seen, so that the sheep, always eager for salt, would eat any sprouting thistles. When the weeds were found to have started in a cultivated cornfield, they were carefully dug out with a spade in an effort to exterminate every root. The farm never stayed completely free from Canada thistles for long at a time, but seldom did a patch manage to spread over a spot more than ten feet square before it fell under attack.

"I have always hoped," Father said to me more than once, "that I might live through a year when no weed went to seed on these hundred and twenty-five acres." That hope he never realized, although few farms were kept cleaner. Weeds were no mere obsession with him. Even today their cost, in terms of reduced agricultural production and labor to combat them, is officially estimated at five billion dollars a year, a billion more than the cost of insect damage. Had Father lived until the appearance of 2,4-D and the other modern chemical weedicides, I suspect that he might have chosen a later period as his Golden Years.

The only time I ever challenged his attitude toward weeds amused him immensely. Potatoes, growing on the site of a fertile old feedyard, by late July after a wetter and busier-than-usual summer had become infested with a luxuriant crop of the quick-growing tall annuals that we called pigweed and lambs-quarter. Father assigned me one forenoon to pull them out. They were well rooted and not easy to lift. I was perspiring freely and grunting with every yank. The sun rose higher and the humidity grew no less. As I straightened up to rest my back and to survey the several rows yet to be cleared, I was struck by an observation that seemed to have important possibilities. Father was fixing a fence nearby, and I asked him to come over.

"Look!" I said. "We ought not to pull these weeds. Where the weeds are biggest is where the potatoes are best. The weeds must be good for the potatoes."

When he was through with laughing, Father said I had made a correct observation but had drawn a wrong conclusion.

"The potato vines and the weeds have both made their best growth here because this part of the patch, where the feedyard used to be, is best supplied with nitrogen. Go ahead and pull the weeds! They will steal from the potatoes, and won't bear anything we can eat or sell!"

I finished the job.

Through the hot and busy, yet more leisurely, August days we heard the cicadas shrill and as the month advanced listened for the first katydid. "Six weeks until frost," we quoted then without believing. Frost had been known to come in August or could delay until in October.

The corn had tasseled out, the silks had appeared, and the pollen had fertilized the ears. As the month came to its close, the outer ends of the milky grains dented and hardened. The once delicately glossy silks dried. The time to cut corn came close. That was foremost among the harvest labors of autumn, also a season of fairs, of special aromas, and of the deep satisfactions to come when the fruits of a good year were gathered.

100

Chapter 8

Corn Knife and Husking Peg

We looked forward to no three-day weekend as September approached. Labor Day was only something we read about. Someone usually mentioned the date at the noonday table. "This is Labor Day." Another might respond, "Every day is Labor Day here." We had our well-seasoned little jokes.

Now was the beginning of corn-cutting time. In some years corn was ripe enough by the last week in August to begin with a few "half-shocks." Labor day usually found the job started in earnest.

Cutting corn was a hard-work job; no one pretended that it was not. But in those days it had to be done, we thought, so that the fodder stalks could be saved for feed, and we did it to the last stalk.

The tools were simple. Each worker had a machete-like knife about sixteen inches long and three inches or less wide, with a thin, not too heavy blade and a wood handgrip. One could use any corn knife, but each person came to like his own. It was kept well sharpened.

Then one had to wear a "sleeve." The sleeve was made preferably from the denim of an old jacket or pair of overalls. It fitted over the left arm, covered the shoulder well, and was fastened to the shirt with safety pins. A piece of heavy stocking with a thumbhole was sewn on the lower end. The sleeve protected the arms and wrist from the sharp and raspy corn leaves and, equally if not more important, saved wear on the shirt.

His sleeve in place and knife in hand, the corn harvester walked into the ripest edge of the field. If he intended to cut "10 × 10," he counted five rows from one edge and five rows in. He caught the fifth and sixth hills of the fifth and sixth rows and twisted and tied the upper halves of the stalks together into a "gallus," a sort of tepee-like frame. He slashed an armload of stalks from each side and set them up straight against the "gallus" so that four armloads leaned against each other. If the corn was still a little green, he would cut only two or four rows, and leave these to dry for a week or so before finishing the shock. In that event he tied the tops together with a cornstalk. When a shock was finished, it was tied by two cornstalks. An experienced man could select suitable stalks, break them carefully between each pair of joints, tighten the top of the shock, and pull it up firmly and tie the ends of the two stalks together so that the shock would stand, if necessary, until spring. If one man had to undertake a field alone, he likely made the shocks smaller.

Cutting "10 × 10" meant ten hills or ten steps each way. A poor crop with short, thin stalks could be cut 12 × 12, and extra-big and heavy corn might be cut 8 × 10 or even 8 × 8.

One quickly learned how to seize several stalks at once in the crook of his left arm and to whack them off with a single knife-blow without endangering his knees or shins. The butts were allowed to drop to the ground, and the armload was increased until one could drag no more. Then he lugged it to the shock, set it carefully upright and went back for another load.

A favorite method was to railroad. One tied his galluses all the way across the field, and then cut straight along from shock to shock, one row across and one back, until the shock-row was finished. When two men were working together, one on each side, the work went right along; neither wanted to be left behind.

September days could be quite as hot as midsummer, and tall corn obstructed all the gentler breezes. Pollen from the dry tassels had a way of dribbling down one's neck, no matter how carefully a bandanna had been knotted. As autumn advanced and as the leaves grew drier their edges sawed, gently but persistently, at the back and side of the neck and at the left wrist where the piece of stocking began to wear out. It could be a little more than dismaying to realize that acres and acres of stalks remained to be cut and that only by slashing away, one, two or three stalks at a blow, could the task ever be brought to a finish. A 20-acre field could contain nearly a quarter of a million stalks. On cool mornings one's clothes were half saturated with dew. On hot afternoons they were entirely saturated with perspiration. When wilted by early frosts, the stalks became drier and more brittle and dustier and the edges of the leaves grew sharper. Corn cutting took the joy out of brilliant September mornings. But it had to be done, so we kept on slashing until all the corn was in the shocks.

Forty shocks were a good day's work. Now and then Father hired extra help. Usually the extra men were paid by the shock, and made a little more than the common day wages, which probably then averaged $1.50 for ten hours.

Frank Kahler, a neighbor eastward from us, was reported once to have hired a stranger to cut corn at a nickel a shock. Frank figured that he would have to expend at most about two dollars a day. The man started at daylight and cut furiously until dark for three days, pausing only for his meals and an occasional swig from his water jug. Frank found that the man was cutting not forty but eighty shocks a day and earning not $2.00, a reasonable wage for heavy work, but $4.00. "I had to let him go," Frank said. "I couldn't afford to pay no man $4.00 a day to cut corn."

Corn grew taller then than now. Science has taught farmers that higher yields of grain, the essential part of the crop, can be produced on smaller stalks. Our seed corn, chosen for big, long ears, most often had come from tall and heavy stalks. If we found a towering stalk, fourteen or sixteen feet high, we sometimes lashed it to a fence post to admire and talk about.

As the fertility of the farm increased and the corn grew taller, it became more difficult to tie the shock firmly. We learned to use a hardware store gadget attached to a ten-foot rope. By pulling on the rope with his weight, a man could tighten up the shock, loop the rope over the gadget so it would hold, and then two men could tie two stalks together in the usual fashion. If they did not break, as sometimes they did, the pressure after the rope was removed would hold the tie firmly.

Before corn cutting could be finished, the time to sow wheat would come. Perhaps an oats field had already been plowed for wheat. Otherwise one of the cornfields was disked thoroughly. The disk and then the drill could go straight between the rows of corn shocks but had to weave around the shock rows. By the time the corn was husked and the shocks taken off, it would be too late to seed the spots they had occupied. The next summer a wheat field stood golden yellow with little green islands of weeds where the shocks had stood.

The corn binder came into use around 1900, and a neighbor had bought one. Father experimented by hiring the neighbor to cut a field or so. It saved many days of arduous slashing. The bundles, green and heavy, were dropped on the ground. To pick up and carry a few thousands of them to the shocks was no easy day's toil, and the binder knocked hundreds of ears off the stalks. After its work was finished, we had to drive a wagon through the field and pick up the fallen ears one by one. It was better, Father decided, to stick to the old-fashioned system, and most of the neighbors came to think the same.

Always open-minded toward new and better ways, Father was not always the first to buy a new kind of machine or to adopt a new practice, although he was prompt to observe and study it. He was one of the first in Hardin County to grow alfalfa. He and Sam Phillips together owned the first manure spreader in our neighborhood. I believe he was the first to buy a corn shocker.

Although he never complained about hard work, he probably did not like the laborious task of cutting corn by hand any better than did, for instance, his son. He thought the corn binder saved no work. In the fall of 1905 he invested in a corn shocker, apparently convinced that it could save both time and effort.

This cumbersome machine combined three kinds of

devices, and required three good horses to pull it. It was the farm implement industry's last major effort to take the handwork out of the corn harvest until, many years later, the tractor-operated picker proved to be successful.

Like the binder, the shocker had two pointed, slanting fingers which picked up fallen stalks and guided the row to the fast-moving mower-type knife that severed them. The stalks were carried upright by endless chains from the knife to a revolving platform upon which the entire shock was formed. When the platform was filled the team was halted and the shock tied at the top by hand with twine. By the aid of an overhead crane, a hand-turned crank and an arrangement of rope and pulley lifted the entire shock a few inches until the butts cleared the platform; then it was swung backward until it was suspended in the air at the rear of the whole apparatus. At that point a trip was pulled, the shock dropped to the ground, and the crane returned its various supporting devices to the platform. About the most that could be said for the shocker was that it worked most of the time. When a field was finished, the shocks stood close together in rows so that the wheat drill did not have to weave in and out among them. But the revolving platform twisted the shocks so much that they tended to settle in a swirled position and were hard to tear apart at husking time, and the machine knocked off nearly as many ears as did the corn binder. After several seasons, when it began to get out of order, Father decided that to make repairs would not be worthwhile.

In fields where the cornstalks stood straight, a far more simple device worked best of all. Two oaken 2 × 6 planks were fastened together for runners and a V-shaped platform was built that slanted rearward to a five-foot width. On each side an old crosscut saw, its steel upper edges ground knife-sharp, was bolted. A steady horse, one that knew how to walk straight and to start and stop not too abruptly, furnished the power. Two men, standing back to back on the sled, caught the cornstalks in their arms as the sled blades severed them, and had only to carry their load a few steps at each shock. If the corn stood well and if the ears did not hang too high, two men with such an outfit could put up more shocks in a day than by any other means. The work was not light, but it was easier than swinging a corn knife.

The clover seed ripened while the corn harvest was still under way. After the hay had been cut in June, the red clover started growing again and by late summer became a beautiful field of purplish-red blooms, without the tall springtime weeds that usually disfigured the earlier hayfield. Whether the blossoms "filled" or not then became a matter of suspense. When the first heads had turned brown, Father would pluck a few, grind them in his palm, and count to see how many seeds he could find after gently blowing off the chaff. If the number looked promising, the field was mowed for seed. If not, and we were short of hay, a light hay crop might be taken off; but more likely it would be left for plowing under.

Machinery for cutting clover seed was less than perfect. Father and Sam Phillips, the progressive neighbor with whom he had jointly purchased the manure spreader, somewhere found and bought an old grain reaper of a type that had preceded the binder. It

107

had a cutter bar and knife like those on a mowing machine. Back of this was a smooth platform shaped like a third of a pie. Three sweeps were so mounted and geared that at intervals one of them raked the clover off the platform into a small heap at the rear. This contraption worked after a fashion for a year or two until the gears became so worn that the sweeps were useless, although the mowing mechanism still worked well enough. Father was not to be stumped. One rainy day he sawed, whittled, and shaved at wood in the workshop. He grinned and refused to explain what he was doing. It was to be a surprise, he said. His finished product somewhat resembled one of the sweeps, except that it had a long handle. Then be bolted a second seat at the edge of the reaper platform. After this was completed, he invited me to occupy the seat and to accompany him to the clover field. Instructing me as to what he expected, he put the new tool in my hands and started the team. All I had to do was be the sweeper and rake the clover from the platform whenever enough had acumulated to make a fair pile. The surprise worked all right, and so did I; but I thought it was a pretty hard and monotonous job. By the next year there appeared a simple bunching device that could be attached to the cutter bar of an ordinary mowing machine. The reaper was sold for junk with my hearty approval.

Once the clover was cut and bunched, it had to be dried thoroughly. At least once and, if rains came, perhaps several times, the bunches were lifted and turned with pitchforks. Finally the thresherman came with his traction engine and the huller, a smaller separator than was used for grain. One or two neighbors brought their teams. Wagons were not liked for hauling clover seed. The teams were hitched to "mud boats" so that the clover could be loaded with a minimum of lifting and handling. A peck of the beautiful little seed from an acre was considered to make the effort worthwhile. A bushel and a half was a tremendous yield, worth six or eight and some years twice as many dollars per bushel. Hulling clover was a dusty job that no one minded much because the work was light, took but a few hours, and could be done only on a pleasant early autumn day.

After wheat was sown and clover hulled, effort was concentrated on completing the corn harvest. The ears had to be husked off the stalks and put into the cribs, and the fodder prepared for winter use. Some farmers referred to the process as "shucking," but we thought that term incorrect.

As for most farm tasks except pulling weeds, some equipment was required. The first essential was a husking peg. The best peg consisted of a stout steel shield to which a steel hook was firmly riveted. This fitted into the center of the palm. The shield was attached to a small leather harness that buckled around the back of the hand. Another type of husking peg, good enough for boys and liked by some farmers, was a simple flat, pointed strip of steel worn across the inside of the palm and fastened to the hand by leather loops around the fingers.

The other required equipment was a supply of "fodder strings." These were sections of sisal binder twine about three feet long. Knots were tied at the ends to prevent unravelling. A careful farmer treated his fodder strings with a tar preparation to make them more weather resistant. He tied the knots after supper in the kitchen. Such an easy sitting-down task need not consume valuable daylight hours.

With husking peg adjusted and fodder strings within reach, one broke the stalk tie around the top and laid the entire shock, an armful at a time, in one horizontal pile, the butts next to the spot where the shock had stood. Bending or squatting over the pile, with the left hand he seized an ear and with his right pulled the peg quickly across the middle of the ear in such fashion as to strip the husks clean from one side. The right hand then grasped the top of the half-bared ear while the left yanked down the remaining husks. The left hand in the same downward movement closed around the shank and held firmly at the base. While the right hand pushed leftward, the left hand pushed a little to the right in a movement that snapped the ear from its shank. The right hand, still holding the ear at the top, gave it a fling to the spot where the shock had just been standing. All that was necessary to husk out the year's crop was to keep repeating these motions enough thousands of times until the last ear was tossed to its pile.

By the time nearly a bushel of ears had been husked, the empty stalks at one's feet had accumulated until it looked as though there were too many for one fodder string to encompass. One picked up a string, stooped over, reached under and around the stalks and tugged until the two ends of the string overlapped. The ends were then tucked under in a manner that, with the outward pressure of the fodder, made a firm and tight band. The knots kept the ends from slipping apart. No new knot was tied; only a rank amateur would have done that. The tucked tie made it easy, when the fodder bundle was thrown into a manger later on, simply to

110

yank one end of the string to free the whole bundle. The string then was hung with others on a convenient nail, to be saved for tying bundles again another autumn.

The husker might choose to kneel on his bundle of fodder, or even to sit on it, just so he kept steadily husking until the shock was finished and all the fodder tied. That done, he picked up the scattered ears and rounded the corn pile neatly so that no greater number of ears than necessary touched the ground. He would have from two to four bushels of corn in the pile, and as many or more bundles of fodder lying nearby.

By the time several shocks had been husked out, he might wish to stretch his legs a little. So he carried the fodder bundles to a central point. No particular rule governed the number, although an orderly farmer naturally used the same number throughout his field. The fodder shock could be small, with only four of the original corn shocks combined, or it might be big, with eight or ten. Whatever the number, he set the bundles upright and firmly against each other. At the end of the day he would throw a tie rope around each shock and pull the tops together tightly. Sisal binder twine was then used to tie them up, for the stalks would have become too dry and brittle for that purpose. After the grain was cribbed, the fodder was hauled to the barn and fed to cattle and sheep. The feeding value was not high, though the animals would pick off all the leaves and often the husks, leaving each stalk bare and shiny.

If two men were husking at the same time, they often worked together on opposite sides of the same shock for sociability. If both were righthanded, it tended to slow one up because he had to throw the ears over his left hand. The time lost amounted to only a few

111

minutes a day, but it was awkward. Two men could divide a shock, however, and both could then toss righthanded. The more efficient method was for each man to work at his own shock.

At day's end the piles of ears were usually left on the ground. A few days of exposure to sun and air helped to cure the ears after their release from the tight husks. On Saturday, however, or sooner if the weather looked threatening, they were hauled to the crib.

By this season the wide hay rack had been lifted off the wagon and stored for winter, and the tight narrow wagon box with extra high sideboards had been fitted in its place. A scoop board, hinged at the bottom, covered the rear end, fastened with long hooked rods that at the proper time could be adjusted to let the scoop board down. If a wagon box had no scoop-board equipment, a wide board five or six feet long, one end over the back of the box and the other resting on the bottom, was put in place before the corn was loaded.

Father always added a bushel potato crate to this equipment for a special purpose. Two split-oak bushel baskets were dropped into the wagon. Then all was ready to bring in the corn.

The wagon was stopped by one of the piles, and the lines tied to the side of the box where they could be reached quickly if the horses were seized with any independent notions. The baskets were set on the ground, and we knelt to pick up the ears. One never could quite decide whether it was more efficient to try to pick up a double handful of five or six ears, some of which were likely to slide out of hand, or to pick up only three or four at each reach and be certain to get them all in the basket. The moment a basket was filled, one leaped

112

up to empty it into the wagon while the other kept filling the second basket.

Now and then Father's eye lighted upon a big, well-rounded ear with straight rows and long grains. After twisting to see that it was solid, he laid it aside to go into the potato crate. By the time husking was finished, he would have filled several crates. Then he would sort the ears over again. The best ones he finally laid on that special rack in the storeroom over the kitchen where they kept dry and unharmed until seed-testing time came.

When no more ears could be made to stay on the wagon, we rode to the crib and stopped so that the rear of the wagon was a foot or so back of one of the four-foot-square openings under the crib's eaves. The scoop board was let down; it hooked just short of lying parallel with the wagon box floor. Then with a short-handled, wide-mouthed, flat scoop shovel that held a peck of ears at a time, one began the rhythmic, back-achy job of tossing the load into the crib. Only an ambitious, tough, and stout man could throw off a whole load without stopping to rest.

One load off, we went for another. To leave a pile of corn in the field over Sunday and run the risk of rain was bad management. Occasionally we woke up on a November morning to find that a surprise snowfall had covered everything during the night. The snow did not hurt the corn, and, if necessary, we brushed it off and hauled it to the crib without waiting for the sun; after all, more snow might fall! An autumn of early snows could compel husking in the fields while the white stuff covered the ground and shocks. With warm foot-covering it was not unpleasant, although one's hands did get cold. If the weather grew too cold for comfort in the field, we could always load the shocks on a sled and haul them to the barn driveway to be husked where the chill was less.

The corn "shredder" had a period of popularity during these years. The thresherman owned the shredder and ran it with his traction engine. Cornstalks were fed into the machine, which snapped off the ears, pulled off the husks with rotating rollers, and delivered the husked ears into a wagon. It chopped the fodder into small bits three to six inches long and shredded the stalks and pith into fragments. The shredder husked a large amount of corn in a short time. Livestock seemed to get more value out of the shredded fodder than from bundles, and the shredded remains made excellent bedding. There were disadvantages, too. Men found the task of loading the shock corn on the high wagon racks to be heavy work, and it was not easy to lift it from wagon to shredder. The machines cracked and broke many grains, and failed to remove some of the husks. Farmers had been accustomed to filling their cribs with ears to which no single husk remained attached; they didn't like what they called the "dirty" look. When the later, more efficient corn-picking machines came into use and did the same thing, the occasional fragment of husk was found to do no harm.

The old, laborious corn harvest, stalk by stalk and ear by ear, now happily belongs to history and will soon pass from the personal memories of men. The corn knife and the husking peg will join the sickle and cradle in the agricultural museums. The contrast with modern methods deserves emphasis. We cut the corn by hand, set the stalks up in shocks, husked out the ears one at a time, picked them up in baskets, bundled and shocked the fodder, and then carried basket and bundle one at a time to the livestock—thousands of slashes, thousands of ears handled and rehandled.

Now powerful engines drive mechanical corn-pickers across the fields, removing the ears from one, two, or more rows at a time and conveying them to wagons. Combined with, or built into, the pickers may be machinery for shelling the grain from the cobs, and even for drying it. The scoop shovel has given way to power elevators. Hardly a stalk and hardly an ear need ever to be touched by hand. With his tractors, his four-row and six-row planters and cultivators, his chemical weedicides and fertilizers, and his power harvesting equipment, one farmer today can produce far more acres and many more bushels of corn than the best farmer of 1900–1915 could ever have anticipated.

A note should be entered here. After World War I, and well before that in the more western parts of the corn belt, the idea that corn fodder was worth saving began to be abandoned. Farmers husked the ears directly from the standing stalks, which were left to decay and be plowed back into the soil. The toilsome work of cutting and shocking was no longer done.

Along with the corn harvest, autumn brought its share of small jobs. Storing the potatoes was one. We produced enough potatoes every season for our own needs, and some years we had a few to sell. As early as possible—St. Patrick's Day was about right—a few rows were planted so that flavorsome new potatoes graced the table while the summer was young. When these had been finished, the truck patch began to yield from the later planting. Digging them out for daily table use was

115

done with a fork that bore four long tines at right angles to the handle, like a rake. When time came for the final fall harvest, a wide-bladed single-shovel one-horse plow lifted the tubers to the surface. When all of them had been picked up and crated, someone took the hand digger and searched out any that the plow might have missed.

After the potatoes had been cured and dried in the barn, but well before any severe freeze, several crates were moved into the cellar for easy access during the winter. The others went into the pit. A thick layer of straw, perhaps eighteen inches deep, was spread somewhere in the garden north of the house. On this the potatoes were piled in a conical heap and covered with more straw. Over the straw a foot-thick layer of earth was shoveled. When the pit was opened in early spring, the potatoes were as bright and firm as when they had been stored, whereas those remaining in the cellar had become flabby and were beginning to sprout. Apples could also be stored in this way.

When the husking was finished and the cribs were filled with corn, we considered that the fall work had been completed, whether Thanksgiving had not yet arrived or Christmas was nearly come. The harvest was in. Winter could blow. The farm was ready for the year's short days, the changing weather, the relaxed pressure, and for the speculative enterprise of feeding the crops to sheep and cattle.

Chapter 9

The Meat-makers of Winter

About the first of November Father began paying particular attention to the market reports in the daily paper he received from the Pittsburgh stockyards. Any rainy day then—and on any kind of a day a little later— he was likely to drive off in the buggy to look for flocks of lambs he could buy. Most farmers raised a few sheep, but not many bothered to fatten out the lambs. They liked to sell them to get the cash for winter. By Thanksgiving time he might have acquired from two to four hundred from within a radius of six to seven miles. He could estimate their weights and condition accurately enough to be able to make an offer "by the head," which after an hour of dickering usually led to a bargain.

Through many winters sheep continued to be Father's major livestock interest, and he undertook to pursue every practice that promised to improve the returns. He searched the farm papers and experiment station bulletins for new ideas, and adopted those that sounded useful. He kept a few ewes and raised their lambs, perhaps twenty or thirty, every year. They lived cheaply on weeds and on odds and ends of pasture that

117

would not otherwise be utilized. This little home flock also usually provided an orphan lamb or two that became the responsibility, playmate, and, when sold, an income source for a small boy.

Because ticks annoyed the animals and were thought to reduce the feeding profits, Father bought a dipping vat. The vat was sunk into the ground and filled with Xenoleum, a creosote compound that, mixed with water, killed the ticks. Every sheep and lamb that came to the farm had to swim through the vat. Their better gains no doubt paid well for the labor and for the dip, which he figured cost about a half-cent per lamb; no doubt the lambs enjoyed life better without the ticks.

Eventually he quit buying up the neighbor's small bands. Instead he went to Chicago and bought carload lots, or ordered them from John Clay and Company, a Chicago commission firm. Western lambs from large ranches arrived uniform in size and quality, which the local flocks were not, and Father thought they sold in spring to better advantage. He found, too, that they "fed out" better and made more gains for the feed they consumed. They were better "doers." This, he concluded, was because they were generally better bred, and were less infested with the internal parasites that had become prevalent in most Ohio flocks.

When a new carload of lambs arrived from Chicago, we enjoyed the excitement of driving them from the freight car to the farm. The unloading yard was nearly in the center of Ada. The flock had to be shepherded carefully down the paved street and kept off people's lawns until, after three-quarters of a mile, they reached the open country. During the first mile they snatched hungrily at the dry grass and roadside weeds.

One person had to keep ahead to see that they turned off on no side roads or dashed through no gates into strange fields. Once well started, though, they trudged placidly along for the rest of the five-mile trip.

In the shelter of the barn the lambs had little to do for the remainder of the winter except to eat and sleep. A series of racks, each twelve feet long, thirty inches high and broad, divided the feeding areas into pens. The racks had tight bottoms. Upright slats were nailed to the sides just far enough apart to provide each lamb a station through which to reach comfortably for his feed, while they prevented him from crowding his neighbors.

Night and morning for the first few weeks the lambs received a ration of oats. The tight rack bottoms were swept clean with a kitchen broom; a wide shingle served for a dustpan. Walking backward down the middle of the rack, Father poured the oats from a bushel basket so evenly that an equal portion fell within reach of each animal. After the first weeks the ration changed to oats and one-fourth corn, then to half corn, and by March 1 became all corn with no oats. The lambs ate the grain greedily within a few minutes. Then the racks were filled generously with clover hay. Before the next feeding time the hay would have been reduced to bare stems.

One other chore remained to be done before the lambs were left to chew their cuds. Each of their pens had a tub, made by sawing a barrel in halves. At the barn's center a tank was kept filled through an underground pipe from the windmill pump near the house. From the tank someone carried water until all the tubs were filled. A wood frame around each tub prevented the lambs from getting into it.

Water also was carried to the horses and mules, who drank directly from the big iron buckets. Each might empty his bucket two or three times. No animals were allowed to go thirsty.

Morning and evening the winter chores followed much the same routine. Two cows were to be fed and whatever hogs were on hand received their refreshments. In winter it was customary, before starting at the barn, to scatter grain in the chicken house so the birds could fill their craws before roosting time.

After the horses were watered, they got their grain, in winter usually only three or four ears of corn. In summer, or whenever they were working hard, the corn ration for the horses was doubled or trebled. Their mangers were filled with a generous helping of hay.

Finally the two cows were milked, and a pan filled for the cats. That finished the day. We might walk once more through the driveway to see that every lamb was displaying a healthy appetite, and to listen as the horses munched their hay. The big doors were slid tight and latched. Darkness was closing down, and Mother was cooking supper. A boy saw that the woodbox, built into the kitchen wall so it could be filled from the outside and emptied from inside, was well enough loaded that he would not be reminded of a delinquency. The woodbox was his regular and permanent responsibility.

Father eventually decided to feed steers instead of lambs. The sheep racks were stored in the straw mow, and wide mangers were built along the driveway's side. In late November each year he went to Chicago to select the cattle, or he wrote to John Clay and Company describing the kind and weight he wished them to buy, instructing them to send a "bill of lading with draft at-

120

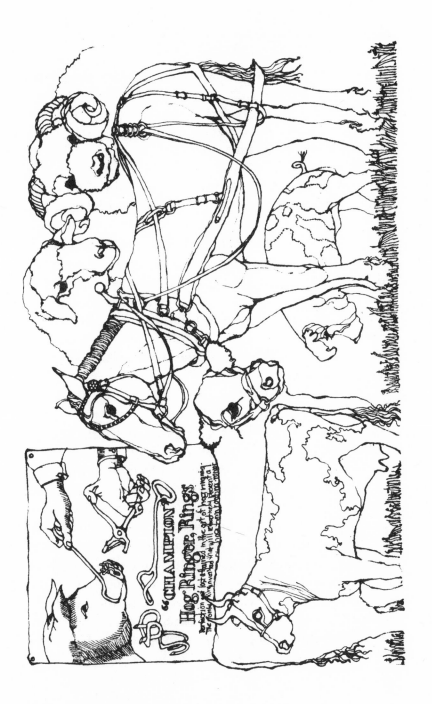

tached." That meant that when the cattle arrived, he took the papers to the bank, which remitted the proper amount to Clay.

The steers came from the ranges, sometimes from Texas, sometimes from Kansas or Nebraska. After some developed shipping fever one year—a sort of bovine influenza or pneumonia—Father preferred to buy northern cattle, steers that had been raised in Montana or the Dakotas; he thought they stood weather changes better.

A carload of feeders included from thirty to thirty-eight animals, depending upon their weights. They would be a year and a half old, having been born two springs previously. Almost always they showed pretty fair breeding, grade or mixed Shorthorns usually. One year the steers were nearly purebred Herefords, all with white faces, and another time they were purebred Angus, all black.

To drive a carload of cattle from the Ada stockyards to the farm was a livelier undertaking than to take out a load of lambs. An extra man or so was needed to coax the new herd through town. Once the stockyard gate was opened, the steers sensed freedom after their days of unaccustomed and uncomfortable confinement in stockyards and freight cars. They were a bit fearful of a man on foot, however, and we took advantage of that. Two men ahead of them, one at each side, and another at the rear could keep them well bunched and moving along together through Johnson street and out to the open road. Once or twice a headstrong fellow might break away and, to our embarrassment, caper over some one's lawn. After the last houses were passed and the country road safely reached, the extra help could be spared. The man in the lead trotted well ahead and the herd was allowed to run if they wished, and generally they did. A half-mile sufficed to tire them and the rest of the five-mile trip home was not too difficult. Only one man stayed behind them. A second moved forward to head off any disposition to turn the wrong way at crossroads or to enter open gateways. Within less than two hours the critters had replaced their lost freedom on the range with a new home. They had the run of the whole north half of the barn. An open door led into a sunny yard with a strawstack at one side. Their business thereafter for a few months, like that of their woolly predecessors, was to eat, drink, sleep, and grow fat. The big water tank set in the north wall of the barn was always ready to quench their great thirsts, even though a windless day could mean that a boy, or a man if no boy was around, had to pump by hand for a long half-hour.

Cattle feeders nowadays consider a silo to be almost indispensable. Silos, if any reader does not know, are structures built like cans—cylindrical structures that tower alongside and sometimes over the barns. Cans they are, in effect. While corn leaves are still green but when the ears are nearly ripe the stalks and ears are chopped and shredded and blown into the silo. When the silo is filled and covered over, the mass settles and ferments. Cattle relish the good feed. Grasses are frequently ensiled nowadays, too, but grass silage was then unheard of, as were the now popular trench silos.

We had no silo. Father was not convinced that one would repay the cost. Instead, twelve or fifteen acres of corn were left in the shocks without husking. Daily a team was hitched to the flat-runnered sled that was called a mudboat. Four or five shocks were loaded and

123

brought into the barn driveway. From this convenient location liberal armloads were tossed into the mangers. The steers quickly learned to hunt for the ears and found out how to eat them. They they picked off all the leaves and most of the husks. Next morning or evening the first job was to gather the well-polished stalks out of the mangers and throw them back under the feet of the cattle for bedding.

When the ground was well frozen, or a good snowfall had come, we could haul shocks on the steel-runnered bobsled as well as on the mudboat. On the first suitable day we brought in as many loads as we could and piled them on the barn floor, so that ample feed supplies would be at hand for Sundays when none was hauled, or for a period of unpleasant weather.

A January thaw was to be expected. If it followed a time when rains or melting snow had left the fields especially soft, the corn shocks tended to settle an inch or so, sometimes even three or four inches, into the wet ground. Then came the inevitable hard freeze. After that, hauling shock corn from the field lost all elements of fun. By then the stalks were either very dry or very tough. No longer could a man quickly hoist armload after armload on to the sled. He had to yank and pull and tear, maybe only one stalk at a time, to get the stuff loose from the frozen ground. He carried along last fall's corn knife to hack off the stubbornest stalks. When a new snowfall clung to the shocks, the frosty flakes were sure to find their ways up sleeves and down necks.

Before midwinter nearly every other shock harbored a family of rats. If the earth from their burrows had piled up inside the shock and had also frozen, the task of loosening the stalks became even more exasperating. The rats consumed and damaged no little corn before spring, but there was not much anyone could do about them in the fields. When one ran out, we tried to run down and destroy him before he found shelter in the next shock.

Rats destroyed grain in the cribs and barns, too. Although traps were constantly set, the beasts were too wary for many to be caught. One crib had a horizontal 5 × 5 stringer about five feet from the ground, under which rats made themselves a passageway. Occasionally, if one had time, he peered through the slats into this passageway and was able with a sharp dirk kept handy for the purpose to stab a rat. One year when a tight crib was cleaned out, seventy-two rats were killed, and many escaped. On another occasion Father and Marve Phillips uncovered a nest of rats in the barn, and a big fellow ran up inside Father's pants leg. Marve's attempts to describe Father's efforts to shake out the rat were vivid enough, although he would laugh so hard that his words of themselves did not help much. He laughed for weeks thereafter when he thought about the lively action he had witnessed.

Nowadays, with the remarkable postwar development of poisons that rats do not recognize as such and devour without fear, a farm can easily be kept free from their destructive and costly presence.

When the barn filled up with livestock in winter, fresh bedding had to be supplied to the animals at frequent intervals. The cornstalks and hay stems from the feed racks were not enough, and straw had to be carried in from the stack in the outside yard.

The steers liked to rub against the strawstack. Within a week or so after their arrival they had trampled down the edges until the stack's shape began to resemble that of a mushroom. Because the exposed straw on the top soon deteriorated, but protected that which lay below, we seldom took any off the top. Below it was too solidly packed to be pulled out with a fork. We had a tool for that, and a simple means to carry a large bundle at a time. The "straw rope" was a light rope about twenty feet long. One laid it down carefully near the stack in a long U so that each half was not more than two feet from the other. Then the straw hook came into use. This was a three-eighths inch iron rod nearly five feet long, fashioned with a generous round handle at one end and a sharp-angled hook at the other. The hook could be pushed flat into the side of a tightly packed stack and turned slightly so that each pull brought out a fair-sized flake of straw. With a fork the straw was piled evenly over the rope. An ordinary pitchfork was too small to handle loose and slippery straw. We used either an old-fashioned wood-tined fork, or a special straw fork with widely spaced tines about sixteen inches long. After enough had been piled, one picked up the two loose ends of the rope, carried them over the straw, and slipped these ends underneath the looped end. Then it was easy to tighten up the bundle and, still holding to the open ends, to carry it on one's back into the barn.

Loosening the heavy, tangled, and packed hay so it could be thrown down from the mows required another special tool. Although one worked from the top down, the first week or so of winter feeding took off all the hay that came loose easily. All the rest had become densely packed. Soon it took exertion enough to bend a stout

126

fork handle to disentangle a small quantity. So the hay saw was produced. About thirty inches long, it had a stout blade two and a half inches wide and a quarter-inch thick. The blade curved backward a few inches and the sharp side was so stair-stepped that when pushed into the hay it cut both downward and sidewise. With a few vigorous thrusts one could cut around a block of hay until he could easily lift off layer after layer with the fork and throw it down the hay chute or to the driveway floor.

The continual handling of hay, corn fodder, and straw tended to keep the driveway littered. Almost daily Father cleaned it with a wood-toothed barn rake, and at least once a week he swept it with a broom. Neatness and order were essential to his way of living. No piles of junk and broken boards were permitted to litter the barnyard, nor were trash and weeds to be seen in even the obscurest fence corners. Tools and machinery were put away properly when not in use. Broken gates and leaning fence posts were promptly repaired. A clean-swept barn was necessary every so often, although new litter was bound soon to cover the floors.

A bunch of shotes always spent the winter in the pens with the cattle. The alimentary systems of the steers left undigested a fraction of the corn they ate. The young hogs grew, thrived, and fattened upon the grain, and perhaps from other elements healthful to them, that they picked up as they followed the cattle.

Nothing except the eared corn fodder was given the steers until early March when some clover hay was added to their rations. Their lean flanks and shoulders would have filled out before early April. The once rough coats became smooth and sleek. The "good doers" bulged at the sides. By the time ten-hour days could again be spent in the fields the cattle were ready to sell.

Father liked to know how his fattening stock actually progressed. He also liked to know precisely what he bought or sold. So in 1903 he purchased a set of wagon scales for $44, which were mounted on clay building blocks over a shallow excavation. Lumber and hardware for the scale rack cost $17.86 more. With the scales hay and grain could be weighed at any time. Livestock could be bought and sold accurately by weight instead of by estimate. During the winter at thirty-day intervals the lambs or steers were driven onto the scales and their rates of gain recorded. Steers were expected to gain two pounds a day, or two hundred and forty or fifty pounds over a four-month period, and usually did.

One of the few times I ever saw and heard Father profoundly angry happened one year when the lambs were being sold. The buyer, a shipper with whom Father had long been friendly, had offered an acceptable price per pound at the farm, and the lambs were being weighed out for the buyer to drive away. Father caught the old fellow furtively trying to alter the scale's balance so that the sheep would appear to weigh less than they did. Without raising his voice, he called the man a colorful series of vigorously uncomplimentary names, adorned with suitable adjectives, none of which I had ever heard him use before. He canceled the sale and ordered the man to leave the place and stay off forever. He immediately telephoned the freight agent to order a car, and shipped the lambs to Pittsburgh himself. Father never tried to trick anyone and was equally determined that no dishonest advantage should be taken of him.

Stock-buyers were middlemen who performed a useful service. They roamed the countryside, buying a few animals from one farmer and a few from another until they had enough to make up a carload. Then they would ship the stock to Pittsburgh, Buffalo, or Cleveland. Competition kept most of them from getting rich. Farmers later worked out a better system by marketing small lots cooperatively. Most of the buyers were honest. They knew the markets better than most farmers did, and managed to squeeze out for themselves enough margin to live without much hard work. Father not only knew the markets, but each year he had at least one full carload. If the buyers did not make what he regarded as a fair offer, he engaged a freight car and made his own shipment. Now and then he went along to the terminal market to see his stock sold. He might ride free in the caboose of the freight train if he wished, but generally he took the overnight passenger train.

If Father ever uttered a boast about anything he had done, it was not within my hearing. Another might brag about his best yield of wheat or most prolific sow; Father offered no counterclaims. But I have found in his diary a few terse items such as "Shipped 135 lambs to Pittsburgh. Topped the market." The final three words were not underscored, but he took a just and quiet pride in the quality of his output.

Always a few animals were left over. A freight car that could hold thirty lean steers in November could hold only twenty or twenty-one fat ones in April. The buyers had a chance at the holdovers, even though the choice main lot Father had shipped for himself.

Driving the fat cattle to the railroad was easier than driving the thin ones out to the farm. They could be expected to run and play for a few minutes after being confined all winter, but they had become too heavy to want much of violent exercise. After a quarter of a mile on the road they plodded along as obediently as a band of sheep.

The barn looked empty and lonesome for a few days after the winter livestock had been sold. The horses were still there at night, and the cows could not go to pasture yet; but the warm fragrance and quiet rustle of a barn full of animals was missing. Their departure meant that the winter's work was finished. It was spring again, time to push on with the plowing and planting.

Feeding the animals in winter, planting and harvesting the crops in spring, summer, and fall, were the most conspicuous tasks each year. Essential, too, were many incidental jobs of day and season, the experiments, and the odds and ends of work; some of these were colorful and interesting.

Chapter 10

Animals, Cranks to Turn, and Buried Labor

The years Father called golden fall in a period that almost completely preceded agriculture's motor age. Except for the automobile, to be mentioned later, no mechanical motive power came to the farm other than the lumbering steam traction engine that threshed the small grain, hulled clover, and shredded corn; that, and the precious windmill.

In preceding chapters I have tried to record, in detail perhaps too minute to interest some readers, what we did and how we worked on a farm that was fairly typical of thousands of others across the Midwest and, no doubt, in other areas, too. Those practices were modern—the most modern—then! Because so many of the once universal farm procedures have vanished forever, obliterated by relentless and fortunate progress, this chapter ventures to report a few others that did not fit conveniently into the chronology of the four seasons.

The windmill was an indispensable. Livestock had to be provided with water, all of it they might want, and no springs flowed on our acres. Soon after he acquired the farm, small though his cash reserve must have been, Father sent for a well driller. The old dug well, although thirty feet deep and walled with brick, was not reliable enough. At eighty feet and six inches the driller tapped an unfailing vein of hard limestone water. The old well was covered by a thick, plank platform, and above it for thirty feet rose the steel tower of the Aeromotor, manufactured then at Kendallville, Indiana. Gears at the top connected to the circular wheel of oblique vanes. The horizontal fan sought and found the wind directions. To put the windmill to pumping one had only to release a lever at the base of the tower. As the wheel revolved, its speed depending upon the wind velocity, water flowed copiously from the well's depths into the tanks at the barn where horses, cattle, sheep, and hogs had capacious thirsts. Their water was never rationed.

Rarely, but frequently enough to keep alive our appreciation for its services, the wind refused to blow. Then the pump handle had to be raised and lowered by muscle power for what seemed always to be an infinite number of times. The imperative necessity that water be supplied to the stock tanks drew exhaustively upon elbow grease. One had time to imagine what a monotonous horror of hand-pumping might be suffered had no one ever invented a windmill. When rising breezes again began to turn the wheel, and once again the task of transporting water could be left to the wind engine, the pump handle was abandoned with zestful appreciation for the inventors and makers of the Aeromotor.

Once a month or so someone climbed to the platform under the wheel and squirted a few drops of oil into the gears. With no other expense or effort for maintenance and operation, the breezes whirled the wheel and ran the pump, winter and summer. After more than three-quarters of a century the same windmill still stands erect and prepared for duty, although an electric motor now substitutes for the breezes.

All the other daily work was accomplished by animal or human muscles. Horses and mules, therefore, were managed with care and regarded with affection. When Barney and Prince, his original bay and gray, had begun to age, Father found a buyer who would treat them kindly, a small farmer whose work was not arduous. Their successors were Ben, a strong, dark bay, and Nora, a capable sorrel mare. Nora in time gave birth to black Dick, who grew into a rawboned, eager, and powerful young horse. Dick was always the first to respond to the starting signal. He aimed to keep at least a foot ahead of any other horse with which he was hitched. "He's like Orange Powell," Marve Phillips said, referring to an ambitious, vigorous young neighbor, "always aimin' to git there first." Ben, Nora, and Dick, with Jack and Joe, the two mules, furnished our field horse power.

In summer the horses and mules spent their nights in the pasture. At six o'clock, when fieldwork stopped, the teams were unhooked from their implements and headed briskly for the barn. They knew the day's work was over. As soon as their bridles were removed, the horses took their fill of water at the tank. Then they hurried to their respective stables. Harness was removed and mangers filled with hay. Each working horse received eight or maybe a dozen choice ears of corn; these they ate before the hay. By the time we had finished our own supper, the horses were through with

133

theirs. However long and hard the days' work may have been, when freed from their stalls after the evening feed, the horses walked quickly or trotted out to the edge of the pasture. Part of the evening's entertainment was watching the horses roll. After a moment or so of indecision as to the spot most suitable for the purpose, each lay down and rolled over two or three times. An awkward horse might have to struggle to accomplish a complete rollover, but if he failed, it was never for lack of earnest effort. After the roll he got up, front end first, shook himself well, and ambled away for the evening's grazing.

Town boys seldom knew that a horse always gets up front end first, whereas a cow always elevates the tail before the head. Country kids considered the town fellows hickish because they were so ignorant about such common priorities.

Unlike the cows, the horses did not usually stand waiting in the mornings at the pasture gates. More likely they chose to be nibbling grass at the farthest corner of the field. Maybe they knew that work, rather than a mere milking, lay ahead. Someone then had to go out with a halter. First he tried to summon them by whistling. Cows, sheep, and hogs were not trained to respond to a whistle; only dogs and horses were called that way. To call a dog one whistled a sharp "wheet, wheet" sort of rising note. The whistles for horses rose and fell softly. When they heard it, they raised their heads, turned their ears forward, and looked to see who was coming. Like as not they returned sensibly to their grazing. At other times, one animal, more amiable or biddable than the others, would meet the visitor and accept the halter. All came along obediently when one was led to the gate; they were sure then to remember that corn awaited them in their feedboxes, and would hasten to the stables. Each knew his own box stall and was resentful if ever placed in a different one.

As long as their work kept them on soft earth of the fields or on the dirt roads, the work horses went unshod. Delivering wheat to the elevator or bringing heavy loads of tile or lumber to the farm over the stoned pikes required a preparatory visit to the blacksmith shop. The leather-aproned smith held the horse's foot between his knees while the hoof was pared and rasped. The iron shoes were heated in the forge, shaped on the anvil, doused in water to cool, and fitted. Nails driven through the edges of the hooves held them firmly in place. After the road hauling had been finished, the shoes, if new, were seldom badly worn. Father pulled them off and hung them up to be fitted again by the blacksmith another year.

If a horse had not been shod for many months, the hooves grew soft. They tended to spread and might split. That called for trimming toe nails. The horse was led to the barn doorway where his foot could rest firmly on the heavy sill. With a sharp wood chisel and a wooden mallet, one could restore the hoof to its proper shape and improve the comfort of the horse.

The pasture where the horses and cows relaxed was covered by thick bluegrass sod that, once uprooted, took several seasons to renew itself. Whenever pigs were permitted to graze on it, they had to wear rings in their noses. The muscular neck and tough snout of a hog indicate that his wild forebears rooted in the ground for a considerable part of their subsistence, and the inclination to root persists in the modern porker. Farmers

135

and animal nutritionists assume that this tendency may be not pure cussedness but a response to a desire for certain food elements that the presumably balanced artificial pig diets do not supply.

Two sizes of rings were always kept on hand, one small enough for little pigs and a larger size for grown hogs. The rings were made of copper-coated wire. The favored shape was triangular, but some were round. One side of the ring was open, and the open ends were cut on a slant so that when the ring was closed, the ends fitted together. A pincer-shaped tool held the rings in its jaw, and a quick squeeze of the handles closed the ring.

When small shotes were to be rung, they were shut into a small pen. One person caught and upended each pig and held him by the forelegs. Alarm and indignation (inpignation?) provoked the pig to squeal furiously, with an extra wail for the one moment of pain when Father set the ring in the cartilage of the snout. Immediately after release his basic good nature returned, and he appeared to forgive his tormentors. He soon learned that the ring made rooting impracticable, although it prevented none of his other customary activities and amusements.

Pigs grew fast, and after they reached fifty or sixty pounds only a quick and adept hand could catch or hold one. Larger hogs had to be held by a rope looped over the upper jaw, or had to be driven into a crate so built that a lever in one end could catch and hold the animal's head.

Though they wore rings in their noses, hogs could be turned into no lot or field until its fences were checked and repaired. Even then it caused no surprise when a patient and alert porker searched out a spot where the wire could be lifted by that muscular head, and usually he was promptly flattered by imitation from his fellows. No hog could be expected to recognize the same opening through which to return; he had to be persuaded gently toward an open gate. Human impatience exerted no influence against the swine's desire to exercise whatever freedom he could get away with, and no conscience restrained his enjoyment of edibles wherever he could find them.

The farm was but once without hogs. That episode may have accounted for Father's lukewarm enthusiasm for larger-scale swine operations. A prosperous lot of shotes had been nearly fat enough to market when, one after another, they stopped eating and shortly began dying. The dreaded epidemic of hog cholera had struck. At that time, in 1902, no preventive serum had been discovered, and no veterinarian could cure the disease. The twenty-eight dead hogs were hauled to the woods and burned on heaps of logs and brush. Not only was the profit lost with them, but for many months it was not safe to bring other hogs to the farm lest contamination remain to infect them.

Except during this interval, three or four sows were bred twice yearly to a neighbor's boar and their litters raised for market.

"Go home and slop the hogs!", the contemptuous cry of an urban legislator to a persistent rural colleague back in the 1920s, gained national notoriety. Our hogs were nonpolitical, but at appropriate times the pregnant and nursing sows and their young offspring enjoyed being "slopped." From the house, vegetable parings, surplus skimmed or sour milk, or any nutritious table or kitchen wastes went into a slop bucket. At the

137

barn we added bran or middlings, sometimes tankage (a protein produced by packers from their meat wastes) and perhaps a dash of mineral supplement. Mixed with water, the slop was poured into sturdy triangular troughs at each hog pen, and was avidly consumed. This old procedure has nowadays been superseded by more scientific feeding methods; but it may be reasonable to remark that farmers who slopped their hogs probably produced more benefits than did their contemporary lawmakers.

The only way a man can get anything out of a hog is to butcher him. He is much the most intelligent of farm animals. As a man is respected in part for his ability to look after himself, so a hog deserves respect. He looks after his own interests so far as to do so is within his power, and only superior force or guile will defeat him.

The cow permits herself to be milked, and the sheep yields up her wool. The horse, despite his great strength, stupidly lets man make him into a slave laborer. The pig allows no such exploitation. He obeys man willingly only as its serves his comfort and appetite. If a gate is opened in front of him, he contemplates the opening, considers what if any advantage he may gain by going through it, and reflects upon the probable motives of the person who opened it. He prefers a clean wallow to a dirty one for cooling off, and is the one barn creature who will not willingly befoul his own quarters. When he lies down to sleep he places his back against the wall so that no hostile enemy can slip up behind him.

Fifty years ago I published a tribute to the hog entitled "The Smartest Animal on the Farm." It un-

138

derwent some ridicule from persons who did not know hogs. Long years later Cornell University published scientific findings as to the relative intelligence of farm animals and placed the hog at the top of the list. Great school, Cornell!

A boy could keep a secret when he thought it prudent. One such secret, never confided to Father, was my favorable opinion of daytime rains in summer.

Ohio does not suffer from the prolonged drouths that recur in some less-favored states. The summer rainfall was not only usually adequate but was distributed throughout the growing seasons. It might rain too often when hay had been cut down and had not yet cured. Showers might come when the threshing rig was ready to start. Those were inconvenient and undesirable rains. The same showers, however, were helping the corn to grow and the pasture to stay green.

Father was better pleased, I always supposed, when the showers arrived in the nighttime. Then they were less likely to disrupt the work schedule. That disarrangement was exactly what suited me best about a good, rainy summer day. Father considered that inasmuch as he could not regulate the date or the hour of the rain's coming, he had best accept its benefits and figure that they would offset the potential damage from an untimely shower. I assumed that because the rain was inevitable I might as well rejoice in its advantages, but I had a definite idea that the less said about this private viewpoint, the better standing I could maintain.

Although making hay or cultivating corn were not exceedingly arduous tasks, they sometimes did become monotonous. Some jobs, such as shocking wheat, became downright distasteful. A rainy day meant a change of pace. Father was likely to have noted a few chores that could be done in the barn, but they were light and easy to accomplish. A real soaker that muddied the fields could also release a few hours for roaming in the woods. If it poured hard and long enough, and the barn and shop jobs were finished, one might even justify sitting down with a book or magazine. The cooling air after a hot spell was a lift to the spirits. After sultry days, a crackling thunderstorm with wind and rain and lightning refreshed both people and crops, and even the tired horses looked more cheerful.

Let the skies begin to clear, though, and the boy was likely to hear a file screeching in the woodshed as the hoes were being sharpened. One could don boots if necessary to wade through wet grass and cut weeds along the fence rows and in the meadows.

"Dull tools make work harder," Father said. I thought that it took a lot of hard work to keep tools sharp. My arm was kept close to the grindstone.

The grindstone came into use to sharpen axes, scythe blades, corn knives, and, most tedious of all, mower knives. My job was to turn the crank and pour water on the stone. Each triangular section of a mower knife had two edges to be ground. Nearly every morning when the mower was in use, at least one of the five-foot knives seemed to need grinding, and likely as not an extra one was made ready. Father knew how to use pressure to even out the blades; I thought sometimes that he must be bearing down with all his hundred and eighty pounds. I shifted the crank from hand to hand, but the stone was just as hard to turn with the left

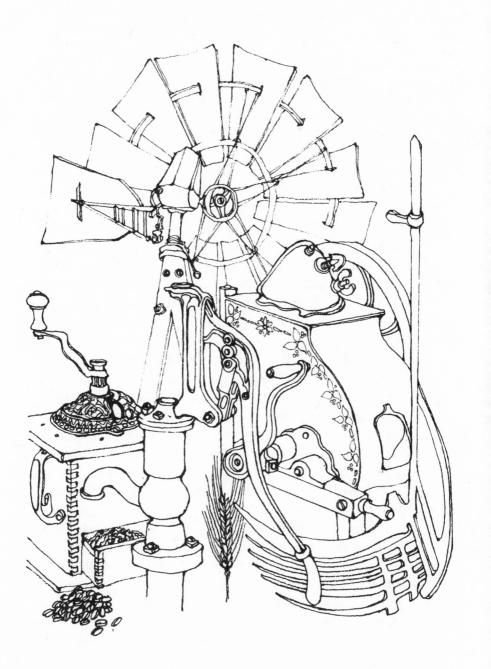

as with the right. Only the good talk that we frequently enjoyed leavened the task with pleasure.

Actually their number was small, though it did seem that the farm abounded with cranks that neatly fitted the arm-power of a boy. The coffee grinder's crank demanded so little power and that so briefly that Mother turned it rather than to try to find me, and she probably doubted my proficiency with so delicate a task as cranking the eggbeater. The barrel churn, however, was mine to turn, and there were times when the butter took an interminable time to appear. Once it was so slow that while churning I memorized half of "Paul Revere's Ride" for a last-day-of-school recitation.

The fanning mill was turned by a crank. Father planted no grain or grass seeds until they had been cleaned. We did not own a fanning mill because Joe Powell always let us use his. The fanning mill was a box-like contraption. Enclosed in one rounded end was a big rotary fan, shaped like the propeller of a stern-wheel steamboat. The crank turned the fan and also by gears and sprockets shook a series of vibrating screens of various sizes. The combination of blowing, shaking, and screening removed weed seeds, chaff, and immature grains. A good job required putting the seed through twice, with the consequent exercise for the boy-propelled arm on the crank.

Not even the grindstone, however, had a crank that demanded as much turning as did the corn sheller. Corn had to be shelled for the chickens, for young pigs, tens and tens of bushels for the feeding lambs, and for other purposes that, as the public sale bills always said, were "too numerous to mention."

The corn sheller was a narrow box about four feet

high mounted on sturdy legs with broad bases so that it never upset. On the right side the crank awaited an arm to turn it. On the left side a large iron flywheel provided the assistance of momentum. A channel at the rear of the top devoured the ears of corn as they were fed into it. Inside the machine a large iron disk armed with numerous protrusions, and smaller toothed cogs pulled and twisted the ears through. The shelled corn poured into a basket underneath and the cobs were carried out through an opening toward the front. One set a bushel basket of ears in the top of a barrel pushed against the rear of the sheller, made a few turns to get up speed, and then fed in the ears rapidly. The faster one could turn, the easier the job and the sooner it was finished. If the ears were thoroughly dry, they zipped through as fast as one could pick them up. Even so, it was more fun to use the sheller for hulling walnuts.

Dry corncobs made the best of kindling for the kitchen stove. At night two or three were put to soak in a quart can partly filled with kerosene. With these as a starter, and a handful or so of dry cobs, a blaze could be set going within seconds. For a quick, hot fire of brief duration no wood had to be added. A corncob of the right size also made a perfect stopper for a water jug. For certain emergencies that might overtake a farmer in the barn soft corncobs were quite as good and easier to find than paper.

The wood and tool shed held a few instruments, such as hatchets and axes, that could be sharpened on the grindstone. A stout bench along the south side was equipped with a strong vise that gripped the hoes while they were being filed and held pieces of wood while they were being shaped with the drawing knife. Sharp files and whetstones lay within reach. Father liked to keep every edged tool in perfect condition for instant use. He spent many rainy hours touching them up so that no time would be wasted when a blade was needed. Each in its proper place above the bench or on adjacent shed walls hung the saws—hand, crosscut, buck, rip, and hack—the pliers, carpenter's square, rulers, hammers, augurs, brace and bits, chisels, punches, axes, and hatchets. Underneath the bench he kept kegs of various-sized nails and fence staples. The wooden maul, steel wedges, and crowbars had their places. Bolts and nuts, rivets, rolls of heavy and light wires, whatever an emergency might demand, could be located. If an item was likely to be needed, he bought it ahead of time. A sixteen-inch length of old railroad track iron lay on the bench to serve as an anvil. It was also good for cracking the hickory nuts and walnuts stored in a nearby keg.

In the light of modern practices, many of our farm's arrangements were faulty and inefficient. The largest corn crib and the principal granary stood three hundred feet away from the barn and feed lots. Corn and grain stored in them had to be carried, usually in bushel baskets hoisted to a shoulder, to the livestock. The wagon shed was remote from the stables. The workshop in the woodshed was even farther from the barn, so that tools and small repair parts were obtained with many steps and the loss of many minutes.

Father had a reason, nevertheless, for these locations. He pointed out that in the event of fire at one building we had a good chance to prevent the others from catching. And he avoided the considerable cost that rearrangement would necessarily have entailed. We walked thousands of steps and carried hundreds of loads that a work-study expert nowadays would characterize as unproductive.

After a rainy spell in the spring, when the sun began to dry the topsoil, Father looked over all the fields to see that the tile drains were functioning and to note whether new ones were needed. Between the highest and lowest points of the farm the difference in altitude was small, probably not much more than ten feet. Water did not disappear rapidly from heavy clay loam lying in such slight slopes. Nearly every year he added more rods of underground tile to the drainage system.

He usually hired some one to dig the ditches and lay the tile, although when no other tasks were urgent we all worked at it. A ditch began at its lowest end, the outlet, which in all cases was a line of larger tile. When this was located by probing with a slender iron rod, Father drove a stake at the spot, tied a binder twine to the stake, and unwound the line in the direction the new ditch was to follow. After this had been staked down taut, the digger began a trench. He pushed his spade down its full length for several widths along the line, then began lifting the earth and throwing it to his left. The normal cut at the top of the trench was two spade-widths or a little more. The ditcher did not aim to lift more dirt than he had to, nor too little to permit him to work comfortably at the lowest depth. When he had dug the first spade-depth for a rod or more, he removed the loose earth that had dribbled from the spade by using a long-handled shovel. Then he deepened the trench by a second full cut with his spade and again removed the loose earth. The outlet sometimes required a third or even fourth cut. Another tool came into use when the full depth had been reached. This, a sharpened semi-cylindrical scoop angled on a long handle, rounded the bottom of the trench so that the lengths of cylindrical tile could fit snugly and firmly into their resting place. As the trench progressed backward, the bottom of the ditch had to rise ever so gently so that water would flow downward toward the outlet. The ditch usually continued back until the slope brought it within fifteen or eighteen inches of the surface, safely below plow depth. Ditching was best done in the spring when enough water seeped into the trench to prove that the level was correct. If soil water was insufficient, enough was poured from buckets to determine that the fall was right.

The tubular baked clay tiles were shaped in diameters from four inches upward. They were hauled by wagon from the tile yards in Ada or Alger and distributed along the prospective ditch lines. When the trench was completed, the scoop had properly shaped the bottom, and water flowed smoothly along the full length, the time had come to lay the tile. If Father did not do this himself, he watched it done. Hammer and cold chisel broke an opening into the outlet tile and broken pieces were laid over the connection to prevent soil from sifting into it. Then the orange-red tiles, each a foot long, were laid end-to-end in the trench bottom, and the earth was heaved back over them.

A meticulous farmer kept a map that showed the location of each line of tile. However, after a summer rain it was not hard to tell where they had been laid; the earth over the drains dried first. Year after year the tile lines carried surplus water away quickly, and not only permitted better plowing and cultivation but saved crops from the "wet feet" that could drown their root structures and hamper their productiveness.

The motorist who views the old stone fences of New England often marvels at the stupendous amount of back-breaking labor that went into gathering the thousands of rocks from the fields and setting them into fences. To some degree he appreciates the toil and trouble that preceded the generous agricultural output of the Northeast's productive old fields. The same observer in the Middle West seldom realizes that a comparable amount of arduous manual work has been exerted to bury thousands of miles of drainage tile in order that the fields may do their best. The stone fences are visible, but the tiles are hidden underground. Nowadays, however, machines dig the ditches.

When a company with a factory in Findlay, thirty miles to the north, offered our neighborhood farmers contracts to raise sugar beets, few were willing to try so unfamiliar a crop. Although Father never experimented rashly, he decided to venture three acres. He sowed the new crop in the alfalfa sod field that was ready to be plowed up that year.

The beets did well, but they required kinds of work to which we were not accustomed. After sowing, they had first to be "chopped" with a hoe so as to leave six or eight inches between plants. Then the remaining hills had to be thinned by hand, which meant crawling on hands and knees over the whole three acres. Next came another three-acre crawl to clean out all the weeds. Finally, in the fall, after the roots had been plowed out, we had to go over the fields on our knees to slash off the tops with a knife. Then they were still to be picked up, loaded on the wagon, hauled to town, and pitched into a freight car.

Crawling on hands and knees was not our kind of farming. Father did not complain—he never complained about work that had to be done—but he did not like it very well either. How well the beets paid I do not know. Father said that their care and cultivation interfered too much with getting other necessary work done. Anyway, that was the only sugar beet year.

From the year's beginning to the year's end, always there was work to be done. But no monotony ever lasted long, for the jobs kept changing from week to week. Besides, much else was going on.

Chapter 11

The Social Whirl

Magazines and newspapers spoke often and compassionately about the terrible isolation suffered by farmers and their wives. Perhaps somewhere in the nation their pity was needed. We seemed to be too much occupied to realize that isolation was such a great rural problem. With events to attend, neighbors to talk to, relatives come a-visiting, public sales, Grange and church affairs, daily mail delivery, the telephone, and occasional trips to distant points, we never thought that we were cut off from the good things of life.

We did know that people somewhere were richer than we, and perhaps did not have to work so much or so hard, and we heard that many more were poorer than we were. Such awareness did not disturb us particularly. We did not expect to strike it rich and did not know how we could relieve distant poverty. In our neighborhood the range from the richest to the poorest was not wide. The richest people we knew lived little if any differently than we did, and the poorest were never hungry or without clothing. Actually, no farmer we knew about for miles around could really have been called rich or wealthy. The hired men and their families were well fed and comfortably clothed. The farmers we knew who owned the most acres were, it seemed, the most penurious; they may have had more money in the bank than others, but certainly did not share in as many of the available enjoyments.

Among the many social resources, perhaps none gave as much friendly pleasure as did "having company." Year in and year out, invited guests came to our house for Sunday dinners, or we were guests elsewhere.

Sunday was the day of liberty and relaxation. Dinner at noon, rather than in the evening, fitted the necessities of the period. Every farmer had animals to feed and cows to milk each evening. To prepare for an evening social occasion and to drive a horse, even only a mile or so, took time. But after chores on Sunday morning there was ample time to shave and dress, attend church, and to meet one's guests or hosts after church.

The visiting horses were given favored stalls and ample feed. When the guests had put off their "wraps," the women offered to help with the dinner. The best tablecloth, china, and silver had been laid beforehand. Because the hour was later than for weekday meals, the men and children listened eagerly as the potato masher thumped in the kitchen and the women hurried to and from the dining room. The hostess, flushed a little from the heat of the cookstove and her responsibilities, finally put away her apron and announced, "Dinner's ready!"

If a guest were known to be devout, he was requested, after all were seated, to ask a blessing upon the meal. For impatient children there was a moment of suspense as to whether this delay was to be endured and of hope that it would not be too lengthy. At home we did not practice the forms of prayer, and once when Father was requested to offer a blessing, he calmly asked to be excused.

The company menu offered few surprises. Home-produced foods, according to the season, were expected. A "boughten" menu would have been considered inferior, extravagant, or pretentious; the hostess would have apologized. Chicken was most often the central dish, fried from July into autumn, or thereafter stewed with dumplings. Fried chicken everyone ate "by hand." Mashed potatoes, and sometimes also sweet potatoes, came with abundant resources of gravy. All the food, usually including the dessert unless that was homemade ice cream, was placed on the table. One might expect green peas in early summer, berries, roasting ears, green beans, Kentucky Wonder beans, ripe tomatoes raw or stewed, leaf lettuce, cole slaw, apple sauce, two or more kinds each of pickles, preserves and jellies, a white cake and a dark one, a fruit pie, and a soft pie. Every dish was passed promptly if anyone appeared to have consumed his first helping; seconds and thirds were urged by host and hostess. Homemade bread and butter were taken for granted. If the day was hot, iced tea might be offered in place of coffee. No one drank milk at a company dinner except a small child. The Sunday repast was not greatly different from the daily meals except that the abundance was greater, the variety wider, and a few extra delicacies were set out. The hostess was pleased if a visitor requested one of her recipes.

When no one could be persuaded to eat more, the

table talk ran on for a few minutes and then everyone rose. The men moved to the sitting room or porch, the children went to their play, and the women cleared the table and washed the dishes. A little later the men were expected to look over the host's livestock and to find something to compliment about the crops or arrangements of the farm. Then men and women gathered together and relaxed while conversation flowed at random. By four o'clock one of the men would look at his watch and declare that it was time to start home for chores.

Our neighborhood—which was defined as the area where any of the people lived with whom we enjoyed neighborly contacts at one time or another—extended roughly two miles and a half to the eastward from our farm and a mile and a half west, north, and south. A tiny rectangle of the earth's surface, even a small portion of Hardin County, but we found no cause to complain that it was not larger.

The "center of gravity" and of mild hilarity on festive occasions was Huntersville, a mile east of the farm. There stood the shabby Grange hall, the square Methodist church, Josiah Smith's blacksmith shop, and half a dozen houses.

Some sixty families lived within the Huntersville neighborhood and we knew them all. About thirty of the families belonged to the Grange, and about an equal number attended the church; more than twenty of these belonged to both Grange and church. Those who took no part in either we saw at public sales, in the exchange of work, as we bought or sold livestock, or when we met them on the road or on the street in town. The gossip was friendly, for nearly everyone seemed to get on well with everyone else. No hatreds flourished, and no family feuded with another family.

Father and Mother had joined the Grange in Wood County, and became faithful members of Pleasant Hill Grange Number 598 at Huntersville. Organized nationally in 1867, the Grange is a secret order formally known as the Patrons of Husbandry. Recognizing the partnership of women in farm affairs, it had been the first secret organization to admit women on an equal basis with men.

Tuesday night was Grange night, and seldom did the minutes indicate the absence of a quorum. Because the meetings were made interesting, the attendance was good. The feature, after a brief ritualistic and business session, was the lecture hour. The "worthy lecturer" planned his programs in advance, varied them with assigned talks, debates, recitations, and music. He tried to invite every articulate member to participate in the general discussions. The Panama Canal, parcel post, the trusts, and other current state and national issues were threshed out, usually informatively. One winter the Grange voted to buy a number of basic agricultural text books on fertility, livestock feeding, drainage, and similar practical topics. These were parceled out to members to read and summarize, and then passed around to others who were interested. Many members had good common-school educations, and some had been teachers. Others who seldom spoke were attentive listeners. None commanded more attention when he chose to rise than did Frank Kahler, whose sparkling eyes, slight German accent, intense concentration, and native intelligence always made him interesting. No one laughed when, in explaining the theory of capillary attraction in the soil, he told with vivid gestures how raindrops "periculated" down through the ground.

The biggest attendance of the year turned out for the annual oyster supper, held in early winter. Then, as now, people enjoyed eating in company. One winter, after the increasing English sparrow nuisance had been discussed, the membership divided into sides for a sparrow-killing contest, the losers to eat beans and the winners to have oysters. The sparrows were not exterminated, but some five hundred fewer were around to make nests the next spring. Actually the sparrows were not serious pests although they seemed overabundant. They did tend to crowd out the native birds, and if hog cholera appeared might carry the disease from farm to farm. Father could remember when the first of the English intruders appeared in our part of Ohio.

Grange membership dues were $1.20 a year per person. Members more than recovered this expense by cooperative purchase of sugar, kerosene, and binder twine. Beyond the price of the commodities the actual cost was nil, because Harmon Shroll always volunteered to bring the goods to the Grange hall. He also made the fires and swept. Because he was so willing and faithful, and firmly refused payment for his services, several members argued privately that he should be honored by election as master. Others objected that, because Harmon was barely literate, he was not qualified for the highest office. Eventually he was elected, and served for two or three years. He memorized the ritual, which many masters did not bother to do, and conducted the meetings with accuracy and dignity to the admiration of all and to the surprise of some.

Father and Mother looked upon the Tuesday night meetings as both duty and pleasure, and not to be missed. Though he seldom volunteered to speak, Father took the floor when called upon and briefly expressed his opinions. He served for a period as master. The occupant of this top job was, by local tradition, always next elected to the lowest one; so after surrendering his gavel, Father became the gatekeeper.

The several neighborhood granges in the county were loosely organized into a county-wide grange known as the Pomona. Its monthly meetings brought farm families from the various communities into acquaintance with each other. If the meeting was not too distant and did not come at too busy a time, Father and Mother attended. They always went to the annual county Grange picnic at Lake Idlewild, a small recreation resort near the county seat.

The Methodist church at Huntersville held Sunday school every week, and on alternate Sundays the preacher appeared to conduct a service after the morning Sunday school hour. The minister attended to three other charges besides Huntersville. Usually he lived in Ada so his children could attend the better schools there. On one Sunday he drove the six miles to Huntersville to preach in the forenoon, and then after a hearty dinner at some member's home drove on to a second charge for an afternoon or evening service. The next Sunday he visited his other two churches. I used to wonder whether he preached the same sermon around four times; no doubt he did. Except for funerals he was seldom seen in the neighborhood between sermons.

In Sunday school each class had its assigned row of pews in the one-room church. The room jangled with sound when all the classes got under full steam with each teacher trying to be heard above the general din.

Mother attended the monthly meetings of the Ladies' Aid Society. Members gathered at a home for a brief religious service, took up a collection for church support or for foreign missions, ate refreshments, and spent a few hours sewing and visiting. The sewing was applied to a quilt, which had been stretched over a wooden frame on legs so that the workers could sit close together around it, each working on a particular portion. As the work progressed, the quilt could be rolled on the frame to bring unquilted areas within reach. Both needles and tongues flew.

A time came when the members began to notice that the old church, built orginally of logs and later covered with white-painted weatherboards, was showing signs of decay. They resolved to erect a new structure more suitable for a progressive twentieth-century countryside. The Church Benefit Society was organized to assemble the nucleus of a building fund. Every other Friday night for several winters Huntersville neighbors gathered for a sort of indoor picnic at one of the homes.

"Jan. 21. 51 of our neighbors here for supper and to spend the evening," Father's 1905 diary noted when the C.B.S. had gathered at our house.

Committees worked to plan games, contests, and appropriate entertainment features; other committees

156

planned penny- and dime-catching amusement ideas. Everybody liked and played the card game called Flinch, then widely popular; but any game that employed ordinary playing cards would have been thought sinful.

No one who could come missed a C.B.S. Friday evening. The parties included non-church families, who liked fun whether or not they were concerned with salvation or a new building. The merriment and sociability for a common cause knitted the neighborhood more closely together. When the new church was dedicated in 1910, a good share of the money to pay for it had been ready. Although not a member of the church, Father was treasurer of the society, and gave a substantial sum to the final payment.

Even though the Fourth of July came in a crowded season when the hurry to finish haymaking overlapped the urgent beginning of wheat harvest, the anniversary called for a neighborhood observance. Early in the afternoon the women gathered at the host home to make the ice cream and assemble and prepare the foods each contributed. The men came in time for supper. Small boys ate their shares of the supper and all they could get of the ice cream, but the suspense was not easy for them to bear. Strict custom forbade touching the fireworks until after darkness had fallen. A boy might have been permitted to shoot off two or three small firecrackers before breakfast to initiate the great day; and just to keep him from bursting, he might have been allowed to ignite a louder one at noontime. No more, however, until the dishes had been put away and everyone had gathered on the lawn. No speeches had to be made. No one read the Declaration of Independence. Each family

157

brought its own contribution of fireworks, and under watchful adult eyes each boy set off his own, plus a few, perhaps, thoughtfully brought by some family who had no eager lad.

First the boys were allowed to shoot off their smallest firecrackers. To hear these explode one by one was so much fun that only a burst of reckless extravagance could induce anyone to let a whole bunch go at once. Next came the bigger firecrackers and finally the cannon crackers, which were carried out into the lane or road so as to endanger none of the buildings. When he had lighted a fuse, a boy ran quickly to a safe distance and waited on tiptoe for the great bang. If it failed or fizzled, he left it alone. The rule was positively not to touch after a fuse was lighted; and thus we suffered no accidents. After the last cannon cracker had burst its red wrappings, the little girls, who had been holding their fingers to their ears, could quit squealing and begin to wave the harmless but pretty sparklers that showered colored fires from a wire stem. By this time the night was as dark as it was going to be. The Roman candles were brought out and lighted one by one. A boy held the candle high in the air, his face turned away a little, and described small circles with the outer end so that each of the fireballs that woofed out at quick intervals went in a slightly different direction. To hold it down into the earth and lose its full pyrotechnic glory was a disgraceful piece of incompetence.

Sky rockets were saved until the last. One of the men saw that they were properly attached to a slanting board, touched fire to the fuse, and walked quickly backward. After seconds of suspense, the ball of fire whooshed into the black sky and, as it turned to fall, exploded into half a dozen smaller balls of varied colors that floated slowly downward.

That was supposed to be the final act. No! Uncle Elihu Mathews had been seen slipping out through the dim lane into the road. Uncle Elihu was tall and spare and dark, grim-visaged and solemn. His shoulders bent but slightly under his eighty years. His round beard lent dignity to his countenance. His speech was precise and slow, and when he rose in church to pray or to testify, his voice rolled out with a quiet fervor that left no doubt or question about the firmness of his Methodist faith. Few of us youngsters had ever seen him smile. He was beyond doubt the most religious and therefore, perhaps, the best man we knew. We were puzzled and rather concerned because we were cautioned not to be scampering about until Uncle Elihu returned.

Suddenly the air seemed to split. A crackling boom filled the night with an explosion so loud that our biggest cannon crackers seemed to have been no more than pop guns. As the reverberations died down, Uncle Elihu came pacing slowly into sight. He had carried out his plan to cap the celebration by detonating a sizable charge of dynamite. We suspected that he may have worn a slight grin, but if he did the darkness hid it.

That was the end of the Glorious Fourth, and the next day was just the fifth. One then cleaned up the exploded cracker papers and enjoyed the delicious smell of burned powder while mourning over what a long year must elapse before another Fourth could be celebrated. A forethoughted boy, however, had saved out one torpedo. That was a little paper bag of gravel in which an explosive paper cap was imbedded. When thrown down smartly on a hard surface, it yielded a fairly loud crack.

The original idea for saving one was that when school resumed, three months later, it might come in handy. On the morning of the fifth, however, the sounds of the night before were so delightfully recalled and the danger of losing the torpedo or that the torpedo might lose its noise-making power appeared so great that it seemed best to take no chances. Its explosion provided a final, melancholy pleasure.

One year the men had decided that, because the field work was so far behind schedule, they would not take off even a few hours to celebrate the Fourth in our usual way. Our town, Ada, however, had announced big doings, and Father insisted that Mother and I ought to go. "You'll see some real fireworks," he said, and we did. After tying Old Doc to a hitching post two blocks farther out than usual and reinforcing his light strap with a rope halter so that he would not break away if the noises frightened him, Mother and I found seats in the little railroad park to await the show. After the band ended its concert, a half-dozen businesslike men mounted the stand. In a moment a tremendous pin-wheel buzzed and blazed. We had never seen anything like that. In another moment the whole stand blazed. The pinwheel's sparks had fallen into the crate that held the main fireworks. The businesslike men scrambled down as fiery devices shot in every direction except up. Frank Young, a post office clerk, broke his leg getting off the stand. The crowd scampered to safe distances. It was the liveliest, loudest, and quickest of all our Fourth of July celebrations. Mother and I were home earlier than expected, and told Father that he had been right about our seeing real fireworks.

When the Carter reunions were held, usually at

villages east of Kenton where relatives of Father's mother lived, we went there. Now and then some of them came to visit us. For several years also the Rising Sun school reunion called for attendance. Here former teachers and students of our district school gathered to spend a day. Austin Cooney, a bachelor neighbor who had been a pupil and who was truly eloquent, made his speech of the year. Ears were strained to catch the soft words of Stephen Biggar, a revered teacher of the older generation.

By late August the fair season opened. For at least one day we went to Kenton for the Hardin County fair. With dinner packed in a basket, we left home by seven in the morning. Once at the fairgrounds, Old Doc was unharnessed in a shaded spot and tied to the buggy wheel, where he could be comfortable for the day; he was not supposed to be interested in the sights. Together the three of us looked the livestock exhibits over thoroughly, made our way through the throngs where the new models of farm machinery and the latest buggy designs were being shown, inspected the fruits, vegetables, cakes, and home-canned products in the pavilion, and visited with all the acquantances we encountered. We strolled through the midway and listened to the barkers. We watched men and boys hurl baseballs at the "nigger babies," toss rings at the cane rack, and try their skills with a sledge that rang a bell at the top of a tall column if the player struck the bottom hard enough and just right. We wasted no small change on such matters. At noon we returned to the buggy and ate our lunch. In the afternoon Mother went to gaze again at whatever exhibits had interested her most, or to find a seat where she could watch the moving crowds.

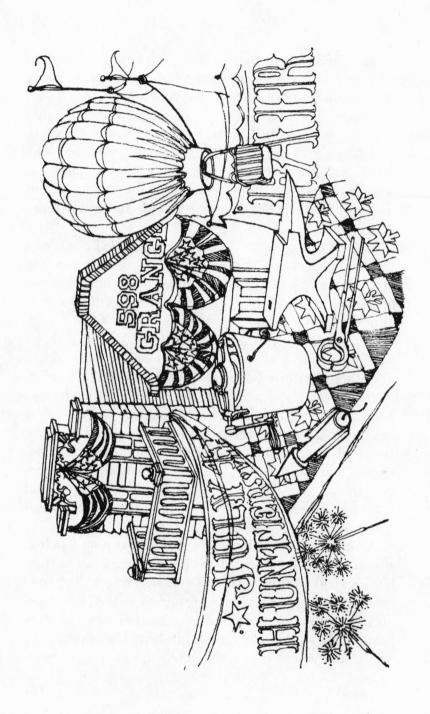

Sometimes I went with her, sometimes with Father while he looked further at the livestock and machinery. When we all found each other again, we looked over the fence to watch the trotting races for a while. We knew that it had long before been established that one horse could go faster than others, and were not much interested to see the fact demonstrated again. Before the afternoon ended I could be sure that the folks would move over near the merry-go-round and give me ten cents for two good rides, or maybe even fifteen cents for three rides. If a balloon ascension had been announced, we waited for that. It was always scheduled for late in the afternoon to keep the crowds on the grounds. After the bold aeronaut had come sailing down, performing acrobatic tricks on the trapeze slung under the parachute, we were ready to start for home. We had enjoyed a full day and, except for the 25-cent admission fee and my merry-go-round rides, had spent very little money.

Father and Mother often attended the Bowling Green fair, which came late in October after school had begun. They went there to visit relatives and old friends in the county where they had been young together.

The Ada Farmers' Institute every winter filled the Whiteside Opera House for two days and a night. The state provided two speakers for an institute in any community that complied with a few requirements. The speakers were practical farmers who were known to have done well on their own farms and were therefore competent to inform and inspire others. Each speaker had to be prepared with lectures on five topics so that he could speak two mornings, two afternoons and one evening. The evening programs were expected to be inspirational rather than merely practical. Father and

163

Mother always attended and, unless school seemed more important, took their son. We carried our lunches; home cooking was better and cheaper than restaurant meals.

Public sales were social as well as business events. They were announced by posters tacked to telephone poles and other conspicuous spots for miles around. They listed the major animals and machines to be auctioned and always added, "Other items too numerous to mention." A sale might mark the decision of a farmer to move to another community or to go into some other business, or might be held to settle an estate. No gatherings were more representative of the whole community and beyond. Father attended many of them, and when the Ladies' Aid or the Grange was to provide lunch, Mother went to help with that.

A sale usually opened before noon when the auctioneer began offering the small articles "too numerous to mention." These often were bargains for one who saw something he needed because the auctioneer hurried along and hoped to create the impression that everything was to be sold cheaply. After a brief pause for lunch, the hay, machinery, and livestock would be sold. Moses McGinnis, old, white-bearded, and sharp-voiced, was the popular auctioneer. He was paid a percentage of the total sales. Each final bid was recorded by a clerk, usually someone from a local bank who knew everyone. Father never bid on anything he did not want, and bid cautiously at that. He was most likely to be tempted by some small item that reminded him of his boyhood, such as two old sickles he acquired at one sale and the candlestick mold he brought home from another to show me how tallow candles had been made before the kerosene lamps had taken their place.

Isolation? Wherever it did exist, that place was not in the Huntersville neighborhood. We had too many friends, too much going on, to be aware of any sense of loneliness. Every day there was work to do, and nothing essential was ever neglected; but we and every other family appeared to be enjoying all the social contacts that time allowed for all the fun that seemed requisite to well-rounded living.

Chapter 12

Educator and Citizen

One winter night while we still lived in the old house, Father invited his five-year-old son to sit on his lap. He produced a book he had bought in town that Saturday afternoon. It was McGuffey's *Eclectic Primer*. The process of education, he thought, should get under way. From a set of alphabetical blocks I had already learned to identify the letters. Now it was time to learn to read words.

He proved to be a good teacher. Within weeks his pupil was able to read all the primer lessons and to spell all the words.

Then came a sunny Monday morning in May. Father stood by Old Doc and the buggy, waiting in the back yard. He was wearing a clean blue shirt, his second-best trousers, and his best straw hat. His blue eyes had an extra twinkle. This was to be my first day of school. I ran out, carrying a tablet and a slate, a pencil box, and a new McGuffey's *First Reader*, and clambered into the buggy. Mother gave me a big kiss and warned me not to forget my lunch pail. That this was an important event in my life, I knew; to the thought that it was also a kind of time-mark in theirs I was oblivious.

Our district school, called Rising Sun, stood a mile south. As one of the three district directors, Father had already met the young lady who had been engaged to teach the six weeks' summer term. She greeted us cordially, promised to make me behave, and thanked Father graciously for pulling the bell rope to announce the beginning of the day's education.

Fortunately I liked going to school. What might have developed otherwise would be hard to guess. Father had determined that his son should have all the educational advantages he himself had lacked. After I had grown big enough to make a hand at the farm work, no matter how badly extra help may have been needed, he never asked me to miss a day of school. I may not have appreciated how strongly he felt about it, but I approved; going to school was always preferable to something like hoeing corn.

Education, in his view, called for other things than the mere formal instruction in schools, valuable and necessary though he considered that to be. One afternoon while waiting for an Ada druggist to fill a prescription, he picked a volume from the small selection of books offered for sale and handed it to me. "I read it long ago," he said, "and I think you may enjoy it." The book was *Robinson Crusoe,* and became number one in my private library. Many of the standard fairy tales and juvenile works of the times never came into my hands, perhaps because Father and Mother did not know of them; but Mother subscribed to the *Youth's Companion* for me, and Christmas generally brought a book or two for my shelf. Nelson Cooney, a teacher at Rising Sun, raised a small fund through box suppers and donations to purchase a small library for the school. Father and I both read all the books it had.

Not long after the new house was occupied, a fat unabridged dictionary appeared on the living room table. Frequently Father asked me to look up words in it, probably hoping to instill the dictionary habit. Now and then he would sit with it in his lap, poring through the pages for most of an evening. His own language was largely free from grammatical mistakes and common colloquialisms, though in neighborly conversation he used "ain't." "I know it isn't correct," he told me once, "but folks would think I was affected if I didn't use their language as they do."

To the end of his life, though, he used an odd version of one word. Whether it was unique to him I am not sure, but I have never heard it from anyone else. When he discussed or announced an action he had in mind, he would say, "I cal'late" to do so and so, instead of *calculate*, the common word for plan or expect.

A book in the little Rising Sun school library fired me up with an enthusiastic interest in birds. From my own small funds, derived from the sale of pet lambs, old iron, and other such sources, I had bought two or three excellent bird books and had learned to identify all the neighborhood birds except a few treetop migrants. For these I craved a pair of binoculars. Having at that point accumulated the unusual sum of eight dollars, partly by working a few days for neighbors, I brought out the mail order catalog one night and showed Father the picture and sketch of the glasses I could buy for that sum. For a transaction of that magnitude his approval was desired. He pored over the catalog it seemed interminably; I thought he must be looking at the harness or machinery pages. Finally he said, "Here is a pair that I believe is much better than those you want to get."

"Yes," I said, "but they cost sixteen dollars. I've only got eight."

"Well," he replied, "I've always thought it would be nice to have a good pair of field glasses around the farm. Suppose we go halvers on these."

He had never mentioned any interest in binoculars, and perhaps had never thought of them. We bought the sixteen dollar pair, and they served well. Long years afterward when I took them to a shop in New York to be repaired, the owner offered $75 for them. "We can't get those good Jena lenses any more," he said.

Our transaction was typical of Father's ways. He never bought anything merely because it was cheap; it also had to be good. And he knew that I would prize the glasses more for having shared in the cost than if he had given them outright.

At that time Marion Township supported no high school. Under Ohio law, however, any pupil who could pass what was equivalent to an eighth-grade examination was entitled to attend a high school to which his township would pay the tuition. The examination, held annually at the county seat, was called the "Boxwell" after the law's author. When I had advanced far enough that the teacher thought the prospects were favorable, Father took a day to drive me to Kenton for the examination and, of course, was pleased that I managed to pass.

I had no thought of going to high school and, indeed, had no idea what a high school was like. Whether Father did or not, I don't know. From amongst all the families we knew, only one girl had ever gone to high school. Passing the "Boxwell," so far as I thought about it, was merely a test. The high school matter was not discussed at home until two years later, one day in my thirteenth summer.

By this time the school laws had been changed. The district schools no longer had district directors but were operated by a township board of education that employed teachers and decided upon the text books to be used. Father was a member of this township board. The Ada high school principal, C. H. Freeman, spent his summer vacations as sales agent for a book company. When he called on Father, he may not have sold books but he easily sold the high school idea. When September came, arrangements had been made for board and room with a family we knew in town, and I was enrolled in the Ada high school. Then, after the four-year stint there, Father encouraged my desire to take some college work. What further thoughts he held regarding my education he did not disclose until later.

Although he clearly approved of the college idea, he handled the matter somewhat as he had the binoculars transaction. When a new term was to begin, he would ask for an estimate of the probable expenses. Not always sure about his intentions and, in fact, not sure about how much he would feel that he could afford, my estimates were always on the low side.

"Well," he would say, "here's a check for half. I guess you can find some way to earn the rest." So, whatever else college did or did not provide educationally, Father taught me to work, and not to throw money around.

Once during the high-school years he took me

171

along on his usual annual visit to the state fair in Columbus. We spent time viewing the exhibits of new farm machinery and carefully examined the prize livestock. He pointed out the characteristics of the animals that made them superior. While watching draft horses being judged, I remarked that it seemed hardly sensible to determine the best simply by appearances. "Why don't they judge by finding out which can pull the best? That's what draft horses are for!" Father good-humoredly argued the question but agreed that it was debatable.

As we walked down High Street after a hot afternoon he said, "Son I'm thirsty. I don't like to drink strange water; let's go in here and have a glass of beer." Eager to see the inside of so evil a place as a saloon, I made no objection. "You'll want to find out about this sooner or later," he said as he ordered two glasses, "so you might as well try it now." After a sip or two I passed the glass to him and crossed the street for some popcorn to kill the taste; but another educational step had been taken.

During the following winter Father approved of my being absent from school on another instructive quest. I had suddenly learned somewhere that the state legislature, soon to begin its session, employed boys as pages at $70 a month. On Friday, as usual, Father had come to take me home from town for the weekend. As we drove along I reported this interesting discovery and told him what I had already done by obtaining two or three letters of recommendation.

"If you want one of those jobs you had better get right down to Columbus and see what you can do," he said. Next morning he put twenty dollars in my hand

and took me to the train at Kenton. "I think it might be more valuable to you than the few weeks of school, which you could make up later."

In Columbus the educational process moved rapidly. The legislative majority was Republican. Our county was represented by a freshman Democrat who, although a friend of ours, had no influence pertaining to patronage. My chances quickly narrowed down to the remote possibility of an appointment by the Speaker of the House. That gentleman received me graciously, read my letters, remarked that I seemed to be qualified and, though of the appropriate age, seemed rather tall. "I advise you to go back to school; if I can find a place for you I will let you know."

That canceled my hopes. I had no expectation of hearing from him. I remained in Columbus a day or so to watch the opening procedures of the legislature and to witness the last occasion, before primaries were instituted, when Ohio legislators elected a United States senator.

Home again, school seemed a bit dull for a few days. Father expressed neither pleasure or regret at my failure. "You've had an experience," he commented, "and probably learned something you would not get in school."

It was for my education, probably, more than for my company, that he invited me to join him on a trip through the Northwest. A visit to his brother, then pioneering in Oregon, was the prime objective of the journey. We went out over the Northern Pacific, and spent a week traveling by stage coach through Yellowstone Park. Motor vehicles had not yet been permitted in the park. After stops at Spokane, Seattle, and Port-

173

land, we had two or three weeks with Uncle Ed at Hermiston and saw how the venturesome newcomers were making the Oregon desert begin to bear riches. Returning, we paused in Salt Lake City, Colorado Springs, Denver, and spent a final day at the Chicago stockyards.

During this expedition Father gave me an unanticipated glimpse at his educational vision. Besides attending college at intervals I had already worked on a few newspapers and had decided that, whatever I might do eventually, I could learn more of practical value as a journalist than as a college student.

"What are you aiming at?" he asked one day as we were rolling westward. "Do you know what you want to do for a living?"

"I want to have a small newspaper of my own as soon as I can save up enough money."

We talked about that off and on for two or three days. He wanted to find out what such an undertaking entailed, how well I seemed to be prepared to tackle such a job, and what results might be expected. I had thought that we had probably exhausted the subject for the time being. But on the last day before we reached home, he had more to say.

"I've been thinking about this newspaper idea of yours. If that's what you really want to do, and I guess it is, you might as well get started at it."

What was in his mind I had no hint, until he added: "I've expected that one of these days you would be wanting to get some more education at one of the big schools like Harvard or Yale." I explained why my plans and hopes were not pointed in that direction.

"Well," he went on, "I have laid aside a little

money to see you through whatever education you might want. But if you are not going to college any more, you might as well take it and buy that newspaper you want."

That newspaper is a story already told in another book. Because a wise farmer-father believed so deeply in education, it became possible for his son, at the mature age of twenty-one, to become editor and proprietor of a county seat weekly newspaper. And that, believe me, really became an adventure in education!

All these incidents and anecdotes together fail to picture fully the manner in which Father abetted and aided his son's education. His example, as he lived day by day in his own quiet, efficient way, stood as a university in itself. Calmly he moved along, through provocations and satisfactions, through achievements and disappointments, never seeming to be depressed, never admitting special elation. He wronged no one. When he helped another, he didn't mention it. He never preached. Living as he did by the Golden Rule— though he almost never quoted it—he did not need to preach.

He took an active interest in public affairs, local, state, and national. His inherited inclination to the Republican party was strengthened by the campaigns of William Jennings Bryan in 1896 and 1900. He thought Bryan's economics were unsound. "Voted for Wm. McKinley," his diary noted on November 3, 1896, the only time through the years when on such occasions he wrote down more than "Election Day."

In general he approved of Theodore Roosevelt's presidential policies, although Teddy's antics frequently amused him. When the 1912 election approached, and

T.R. veered off with the Bull Moose party, Father voted for Taft. The straight ticket, though, was no unbreakable habit. For local offices, where he knew the candidates, he voted his judgment as to the best man. Once, when he admitted having voted for a Democratic candidate for governor, he gave his reason. "When Donahey was state auditor," he said, "he refused to approve an expense account that charged 30 cents for a baked potato. He's my kind of man."

Not many notable political personalities came to Hardin County, but when they did he was likely to attend. One September afternoon in 1908 he and I listened for an hour and a half while an aged, white-bearded gentleman, clad in a Prince Albert coat, stood in the hot sun and took the Democrats over the coals. He was of special interest to Father—"Tama Jim" Wilson, the Iowan who through the McKinley, Roosevelt, and Taft administrations was secretary of agriculture. On the same program a handsome young man in a cutaway coat spoke with charming eloquence for another hour. He came from the adjoining county, and had been our state's lieutenant governor, Warren G. Harding. On an earlier occasion Father took me along to a county convention where the year's Republican candidates were selected, among them Frank B. Willis to be our county representative in the state legislature, from where he went on to become representative in Congress, governor of Ohio, and United States senator.

For many years Father served as a member, and part of the time as president, of the Marion Township school board. Punctually and faithfully he attended the monthly meetings and conscientiously carried out the assigned responsibilities.

One of these jobs was unique. Under the Articles of Confederation the Congress of the United States passed the Land Ordinance of 1785. This measure provided that the land west of the Alleghenies and north of the Ohio River should be surveyed into townships, each six miles square, and the townships into sections of 640 acres each. Section Sixteen in each township was to be reserved for the support of education. In Marion Township Section Sixteen stood in the midst of the Scioto Marsh and was long considered to be worthless. Consequently after all other Ohio townships had sold their school land, Marion still held ownership of its section. Then the marsh was drained, and it became valuable farm land. The school board rented it out advantageously, and the annual taxes for educational purposes were reduced accordingly.

Also for many years he was a member, and much of the time chairman, of the election board for our end of Marion Township. Although his name was occasionally suggested for the board of county commissioners, he never became a candidate. Plenty of competent men, he said, were glad to take such jobs, and he saw no duty to seek a conspicuous place.

Another of his public services took him on two or three occasions to Toledo as a member of federal grand juries. He never remarked about cases before these juries, and probably few knew that he had served. But this, he thought, was a public duty; and when a federal marshal tapped him for service, he put aside other plans and went to do his best. He also served now and then on the Hardin County grand and petit juries, and never asked to be excused.

Although neither shy nor exactly retiring in

contacts with other people, he was anything but forward. He met folks halfway. During World War I and in the period just after, when the government appealed for people to buy bonds, Father surprised many by becoming an aggressive salesman. He felt that the government needed the money its citizens could spare, and believed that if the spare money went into bonds the danger of inflation would be reduced. He spent any number of days calling upon people in the area assigned to him, argued down the recalcitrants, and prodded the delinquents who offered to buy a $100 bond when he knew they could as well buy $2,000 worth. He also worked hard at collecting funds for the Red Cross.

Considering his ardent and liberal interest in education for his son, he evidently had hoped that his offspring might make a special mark somewhere in the world. For himself, he was thoroughly content to try to deserve the respect and good will of the neighbors and acquaintances among whom we lived. Among these many were interesting, some for one reason and some for another. On the whole, they were good people and good Americans.

Chapter 13

Neighbors and Incidents

Only once did violent physical conflict among men create exciting news for Huntersville. The fight was bloody, the consequences long drawn-out; yet no new or enduring animosities contaminated the neighborhood.

The Jackson family owned the largest wooded tract in the vicinity. Two middle-aged brothers, Andrew and Homer, and their two sisters, Mary and Phoebe, all unmarried, lived on an unimproved road near the center of their considerable acreage. Although they attended neither church nor Grange, and shared in none of the community social life, they were by no means recluses. All four were affable and gentle. That they chose to live so quietly by themselves was considered mildly eccentric but no particular business of anyone else. They were thought to be a little old-fashioned—perhaps partly because they continued to use the fireplace in the older part of their house—but were held in genuine respect.

More than half a mile distant Fred Shroll owned a thirty-acre farm that adjoined one of the Jacksons' woodlands. Here he had sired a family of five rangy sons and two good-looking red-headed daughters. Fred and his sons had time to spare, and they liked to hunt.

The Jacksons forbade hunting or trespassing on their lands. This big woods, an ancient home for squirrels and rabbits, quail and raccoons, naturally presented a constant temptation to the Shrolls. The story was that they had been warned repeatedly against hunting in the Jackson woods.

Fred Shroll's sons brought him home one day, bloody and bruised. There had been an argument, and the Jacksons, they charged, had clubbed their father. Whatever the facts about the details, Fred had taken a hard beating from which he required several months to recover.

Warrants were sworn out by both sides. The incident was the topic of discussion for weeks throughout the neighborhood. The talk was curiously judicial and nonpartisan. Sympathy went out to Fred Shroll for his hurts and to the Jacksons for their provocation. The courts evidently took a similarly balanced view, for after many delays and postponements the matter dropped out of sight.

To anyone dependent upon news items redolent of human frailty, the Huntersville area could have seemed to be deadly dull. Not that the place was an absolute Utopia where only righteousness and decency and perfection prevailed; some small leaks in the roof must have been noticed. To whatever extent the standards of respectability were violated, the breaches never were conspicuous. Nevertheless the general rectitude did not prevent a natural human interest in what other people did and what they were like. We talked about our neighbors, and no doubt they talked about us.

Everyone who knew Wallace Runser had something to say about him, and all said the same thing. They said they liked to hear him laugh.

For years Wallace was Father's closest crony. Wallace was sturdily built and corpulent. His famous laugh came easily from down around his diaphragm and rang out, deliberate and clear. It was no rude guffaw nor boisterous haw-haw, but a genial, ringing sound that seemed to leave the air around him ozone clean. Every year he disappeared for a few weeks, returning to tell of experiences hunting deer in Maine or Arkansas, fishing in Florida, or exploring in some other far-off state. The stories always had a humorous turn. He had served in the Civil War and had spent an unpleasant period in a Confederate prison. Occasionally he regaled Father with some laughable war experience but never referred to any serious one except to the bare fact of his imprisonment. He was never the hero of his anecdotes. He never joined the Grand Army of the Republic nor attended the annual Decoration Day services.

As the only man I knew who claimed to have visited every state, he found himself confronted one rainy morning in our barn with a boyish question. I had been saving it up for him.

"Mr. Runser, you've been in every one of the United States. What state do you like best?"

He looked out the barn door at the drizzle for a while as though giving the question his gravest consideration. Then he replied:

"Hardin County!"

His laugh rang through the barn until the horses raised their ears, but somehow I felt that he was not spoofing me. He had seen the country, but the part where we were neighbors was the part he loved most.

He had inherited a good farm, improved it, and added another to it. Though he did less hard work than almost any other farmer around, he prospered better than most. His three daughters and two sons were devout attendants at the Huntersville church. His deceased wife had been intensely pious, and the youngest daughter, Jennie, a handsome, copper-haired woman whose face and figure could have adorned the jacket of a sensational historical novel, spent most of her life with her husband as a missionary in India. Wallace himself never went to church. Why, we didn't ask. No one asked his neighbors such intimate questions.

Josiah Smith, the aging blacksmith at Huntersville, was a fine citizen. Short, muscular, bearded, jovial, faithful at church, and perpetual chaplain at Grange, he had one peculiarity. Instead of saying "Amen" to indicate his approval of a prayer or a talk, he said "Sol-me-do!" As "Sol-me-do" Smith he was known well beyond the community.

Jack and Stimp Bloodworth were the only "foreign-born" citizens of the neighborhood besides "Sol-me-do" Smith. As he had been, they were born in England and brought to Hardin County as boys. No one thought of them as being different on account of their place of birth, any more than I thought of my Canadian-born mother as foreign. They were neighbors and citizens.

Jack and Stimp had other distinctions that were more interesting. Both had been drunkards, and both became teetotalers. Each owned thirty or forty acres and a team of horses with enough implements to cultivate their small fields. Jack, a bachelor, lived in a neat though unpainted one-room cabin across the pike from our farthest field, and rented out his land. A bench under a west window provided him with a bed and resting place where on cold days he could lie and watch passersby. Under his south window another bench held his tools, and there he sharpened the neighborhood saws. A tall hickory tree shaded the cabin. Jack rigged a wide plank with a six-inch block under one end to give it a comfortable slant and upon the same end fastened a wooden pillow, which, softened with an old coat, permitted him to enjoy the summer days in what he considered solid comfort. As the sun made its circuit, Jack moved his outdoor sofa to keep it in the shade. We used to say that one could tell the time of day by the direction toward which Jack's feet pointed from under the hickory tree. Nearby was his well with its wooden pump and good cold water. When working in our field across the road, we found it pleasant to visit the well for a drink and to chat a while with Jack. One day when I tried to draw him out a little about his relaxed philosophy of living, he summed it up briefly: "All I want is a little grub, a few duds, and somethin' for my cats."

Once every week or so Jack threw a grain bag over his shoulder, walked the three miles to McGuffey, the nearest place with stores, and carried his supplies home in the bag. McGuffey was a saloon town, and during his drinking days his walk home was unsteady. Harmless though he was, small children were afraid of him then.

Jack was small and slender. When younger he

worked out at digging ditches and doing other skilled chores for nearby farmers. His full beard seemed huge for a man so slight. Stimpson, his younger brother, was a heavy, powerful man whose long beard fitted him perfectly. Stimp was a widower with three handsome daughters. Besides digging ditches, Stimp regularly hired out at threshing time on condition that he could choose his job. He specialized in pitching bundles from shock to wagon and was generally admired as the steadiest and most accurate bundle-pitcher anywhere around. He had a fixed idea about wages, too—the price of a bushel of wheat, he said, should be the pay for a day's work.

Neighbors repeated a story about an alleged incident when Jack and Stimp had driven to Kenton to pay their taxes. Each had furnished a horse to make a team for the spring wagon. After settling with the county treasurer, they saw that a snowstorm was impending and promptly agreed that the ten-mile trip home in the open wagon was likely to be a cold ride. It was prudent, they decided, to provide themselves some of the interior warmth that could be obtained in any one of the several saloons around the courthouse square. Winter's early darkness had fallen when they started home, feeling gay and brotherly and cheerful. A bit of bantering about their respective horses led to a wager and a horse race. Each took the line to his horse and the beasts were urged into a lively gallop. Inasmuch as the lines were rigged for driving a team, and not for driving separate horses, the animals soon became confused. The story concluded with the report that later travelers found Jack and Stimp sleeping peacefully in a roadside snowdrift.

Stimp's announcement some years later that he was through with drinking whiskey made a resounding sensation. He never explained his reasons other than to say that he had had enough. His general character was such that no one was surprised when he kept his pledge. Jack quietly abandoned the bottle a few years later, and both lived for twenty sober years thereafter.

Their reform was heartily commended. The customs of the community were definitely dry, and booze in any form was considered to be an evil. Social drinking was unknown. No visitor was ever offered a spirituous libation, nor wine nor beer, and none was ever expected. That no home ever kept liquor would be hard to say, but no one was known or suspected to be a secret drinker. Saloons had been voted out of Ada by 1900 and out of the county long before Volstead.

Superstitions were almost as rare as liquor. Now and then someone professed belief in planting according to the moon's phases, or someone remarked that this or that was a sign of rain. For most of the folks such ideas were merely matter for conversation. A boy who killed a snake might be told, as he watched its tail continue to writhe, that the serpent would not die until sundown, but he was likely to doubt whether that really was true. I never knew Father or Mother to pay the slightest attention to any of the old folk beliefs.

Nearly all the farms in the neighborhood were owned and operated by sons and grandsons of original settlers. Runsers owned most of the land to the west of us. The eastern area was held largely by Mathews, and to the north were the Shankses and the Epleys. All of these families, like the Powells and the Cooneys, had descended from pre–Civil War pioneers. The first farmers to come brought little wealth with them. The wealthy, as has often been said, seldom pioneered. The period of less than a century behind us in Hardin County had been too short and too difficult for large accumulations to appear. Other than in farm land, we knew of little inherited wealth. Legacies from one generation to the next were not large when divided among the children; frequently a farmer had to earn capital to pay for the shares of brothers and sisters before he could claim full ownership of his land.

Although the longer-established families predominated, clannishness did not prevail. All treated us as they did each other, as friends and neighbors. Father's character and his ability as a farmer, and Mother's personality, would likely have won them an equal standing in any community.

Those who came first, when the county was new, must constantly have felt the pressure of time. Only by using all the hours of daylight could they hope to remove the trees and stumps and plow and plant new acres. The feeling that work was always urgent passed down to most of the succeeding generations. Only the absolute necessity for physical rest afforded an acceptable excuse for a man to be idle in weekday daylight hours.

This may have accounted for the talk about Shelly Shanks, who farmed eighty acres just north of us. Jovial, kindly, and intelligent, Shelly was well liked. Year after year the Grange elected him as its secretary. He and his family attended the Presbyterian church in Ada, and he was better acquainted in the village than most of us. He often went to town during the week, where he enjoyed visiting with friends in the hardware store and on the street corners. The talk was that he went to town every day, although this was probably not true. It was said, also, that he never went just to go to town; he always had to go after some nails, or his wife Molly was out of sugar, or some other proper errand required the trip. A farmer could not be thought to go to town merely for pleasure. He had to have a suitable reason.

Our nearest neighbor was Henry Hetrick. Henry was a tall, spare man with an uncommonly penetrating voice. Under frequent atmospheric conditions his drawling tones carried easily across the quarter-mile space that separated our houses. In summer he always waited until after supper to feed his hogs. We could hear him talk to them or shout orders to one or another of his children. After throwing the baskets of corn into the feedlot he leaned on the rail fence while the porkers ate.

"I like to hear hawgs chawnk their feed," he explained.

Both our draft teams were helping neighbors thresh one afternoon. Father had fitted Old Doc with some ancient pieces of harness and had hitched him to the one-row cultivator so that we could finish a small job he was anxious to complete that day. The old harness, unused for years, gave way at a critical point and appeared beyond hope of repair.

"Go over and see if you can't borrow some harness from Henry," Father directed.

We so seldom borrowed anything that, though I felt that it was not exactly wrong, neither was it an entirely creditable thing to do. As Henry was laying out the harness I made apologies and explained our urgency.

187

"I don't know what neighbors are for," Henry said, "if it ain't to borrow from."

The only widely famed persons among our neighbors were nearly the quietest and most retiring. They were the Orth brothers. Skilled breeders of Rambouillet sheep, they exhibited their stock not only at the Ohio State and other big fairs but at the annual International Livestock Exposition in Chicago. As repeated winners of championships and grand championships, they were able to sell their animals at premium prices. Western sheep ranchers liked the Rambouillet breed because they were big, and because their ancient Merino ancestry gave them the flocking instinct desirable on the unfenced range pastures. From as far as Idaho and Wyoming they came to Orths for breeding stock.

Of the four brothers, two were almost never seen away from their farm except at the livestock shows. The oldest brother, Alex, came regularly to Grange, but was too shy to speak in any of the discussions, and refused to serve in any office except that of gatekeeper, the lowest. Lewis, the youngest, taught in country schools and eventually married Emma Guider, one of my former teachers. The others were bachelors. After the four brothers and their spinster sister died, Emma inherited their extensive land holdings.

Not far from the Orths one aged farmer held memories unique in the community; he had worn a uniform in the Mexican War of 1846–48. Whether he held any secrets from the Battle of Buena Vista or the Siege of Chapultepec I never was to learn. He died before my curiosity regarding such matters had been aroused.

Neither did I learn until too late that our old log house had produced a mathematician so eminent that

188

he was listed in *Who's Who*. His name was Cornelius Keyser, and he was professor of mathematics at Columbia University. Not until several years after moving to New York did I learn of the man and his place of birth. He replied graciously to my request to call upon him, but before a date could be arranged, the newspapers reported his death. It was from his father, Jacob Keyser, that my father had purchased our farm.

Most all our neighbors were industrious, prudent, upright farmers who attended quietly to their own affairs and lived in their own ways of modest comfort. With no shootings, no feuds, no divorces, no scandals, perhaps their lives and ours were dull and narrow. Even with the touch-ups that distant memory is likely to furnish, one could not picture Huntersville as a highly colorful community. Perhaps that the people were lawabiding, progressive, and decent was well enough.

Chapter 14

Buggy and Model T

Probably it was 1903 or 1904; it could have been a year earlier or later. Father and I were driving Old Doc up Johnson Street in Ada.

"Bang! Bang! Bang!" We heard the explosion after explosion. Old Doc squatted and flattened his ears. Before we could ask each other what was happening, we saw. A topless buggy came out from Lincoln Avenue, a block ahead of us, and turned northward. Two men were riding in it, one holding on to a lever. The thing not only had no top, it had no horse! The explosions continued, and smoke trailed from the rear as it quickly outdistanced us and turned out of sight on Buckeye Street.

We had just seen our first horseless carriage. The automotive age had dawned in Hardin County, right in front of Old Doc. It had dawned with a bang—several of them.

We had read about these machines and had seen their pictures. A year or so later we heard that Charley Cole had taken a Ford agency, and that Dr. Ames had become his first customer. That was no surprise. Dr. Ames was the town's busiest physician, always in a

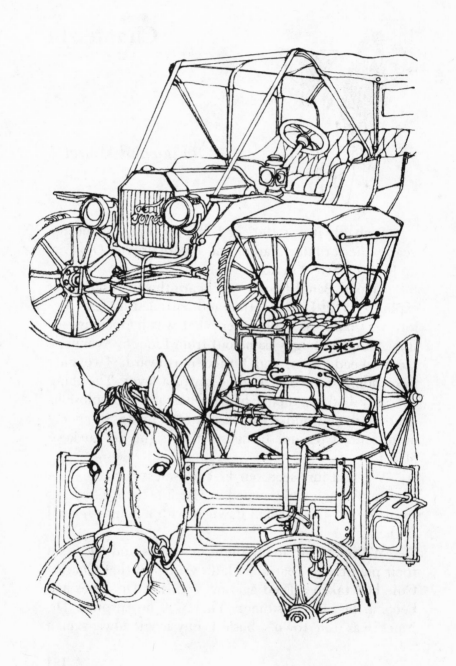

hurry, always absorbed in his work. A young man, Miles Kanode, the son of our first rural mail carrier, had been trained to drive automobiles and worked as chauffeur for Dr. Ames. That was a quite fancy new word that we then added to our vocabularies and pronounced "shawfer."

Almost everyone was talking about the automobile. After all, a machine that traveled over streets and even over country roads without being pulled by a horse was a remarkable invention. Few farmers looked forward to owning one. They believed, as did most of the manufacturers then, that the automobile had a future as a plaything for the rich and perhaps had a purpose for doctors who, like Dr. Ames, were expected to respond promptly to calls as far as six or eight miles from their homes and offices. The combination of the telephone and the automobile, we realized, could save a life in the event of an emergency. Doubters were heard, as always. "I predict the time will come when you'll see one of them automobiles in every fence corner," one of our neighbors proclaimed.

When energetic Danny McLaughlin, who managed to combine being a restaurant waiter and small-scale real estate tycoon, bought the ninth car in town, the Ada *Herald* remarked that it was second-hand, "but appears to raise as much dust as any of the others."

Before long two more automobile agencies appeared in Ada. Mr. Tarleton was attempting to sell Overlands. Otto Stemple was trying to sell Studebakers. I thought it was quite a compliment when Otto drove into our lane one evening and tried to interest Father in buying one. We looked at the car with admiration, but

Father made it clear that he had no desire to become the owner of a rich man's toy.

Charley Cole, the Ford dealer, considered Father a fair prospect and tried persistently to make a sale. But Father was no sucker for every new gadget. He had to be convinced.

"Tell you what I'll do," he said during one of their interviews. "I'll pay you to take my wife and me up to the Bowling Green fair."

"You'll never be able to resist buying a car if you once take a trip like that," Charley warned him.

Father paid Mr. Cole $6.00 for the 50-mile round trip, six cents a mile. But he bought no car just then. That was in 1909. The next year in August the Carter reunion was to be held at Larue, some twenty miles east. Mr. Cole drove us all over there for two dollars. That was my first long drive, and for weeks I told everyone about it. "And we made the trip both ways without a single puncture" was the story's climax.

Farmers by then were beginning to buy Henry Ford's sensational Model T. Mother never failed to report when she learned that a neighbor had bought one or was rumored to be talking about buying a car. After several had become motorists, she began to suggest openly that we ought to buy an automobile.

"Henry is taking $50 off the price every six months," Father would grin. "If we just wait long enough he'll be giving them away, or maybe pay us to take one."

When he decided that the time had come, he gave in to Mother's pressure, though no doubt his own desires had something to do with the purchase. He bought a 1912 Ford "touring car," with curtains that were kept under the seat and a top that could be but never was folded back like a buggy top. It started in response to a crank. On cold days the response came sooner if one had a kettle of hot water to pour over the carburetor.

Two years later, having become convinced that the automobile had come to stay, Father wrote me that he had turned in the Ford and had bought a light Buick. When I came home a few weeks afterward, he met me at the train with a heavy Buick touring car.

"That little one had too much snap and pick-up," he explained. "I traded it for something steadier." He was not a man for frequent changes, however. A few months before his death he purchased his third car of the same make.

The automobile began a new era in more ways than one. The cash cost for transportation rose sharply, and we used more of it. Old Doc, the then new driving horse Father had bought in 1894, cost $85. Through all the years until the car took over his jobs, Old Doc pulled the buggy for every five-mile trip to Ada, for the occasional eleven-mile trips to Kenton, for the trips to church and Grange and public sales and errands around the neighborhood. He trotted the annual eighteen-mile journey to the reservoir and back when we went fishing and made that jaunt other times when Father wished to try his aim at duck shooting. He took us on thirteen-mile rides to Dunkirk when Uncle Ed lived there, and at least once or twice traveled fifty miles to Bowling Green. The vehicle he pulled during his first four years was a $47 buggy, which was replaced in 1898 by a $50 rubber-tired job. He had one new set of harness during his lifetime which cost around $20. Always healthy, he

195

ran up no veterinary bills. No cash was ever laid out for his fuel except on the occasions when he was taken to a livery barn to await the driver's return from some brief railway journey, or when he was put up there to be sheltered from cold or rain while some one attended an all-day meeting. The cost of keeping him in "tires" ran between two and three dollars a year for horseshoes.

Doc was not expensive. Neither was he speedy. His best gait was five miles an hour and to get him to move that fast one had to tickle his flanks lightly with the tassel of the accelerator, which we called the buggy whip. He may once as a colt have been struck hard with a whip, because the very sight of it stimulated his speed. If he had been lashed sharply, he surely would have jumped out of his harness. His preferred gait was about three miles an hour; he didn't mind trotting steadily, but it often appeared that he tried merely to lift himself up and down without reaching out for distance. Doc could never have won a horse race, but he was infinitely gentle and patient and sensible. He was perfectly safe for Mother to drive. When automobiles began to appear on the country roads, he never whirled and upset the buggy or ran away as many horses did. No one had to scramble out and hold his head. As the noisy vehicle approached, whether from behind or in front, he spread his feet and squatted as though to brace himself against being pushed over. Once the thing had passed, he resumed his steady jog.

Old Doc was never sold. The automobile merely relieved him from most of his work. He appeared content to retire, lazing away summers in the pasture and winters in his warm stall. At the mature age of 34 he died; and that day we all wept.

Except on the principal streets of our nearby towns, Old Doc never knew what traveling on a pavement was like. The main roads of his journeys were piked. Pike building contractors graded a strip not more than eight or ten feet wide, and made some provision for its drainage. The width was not enough for two loaded wagons to pass in soggy weather without one teamster running the risk of getting outer wheels stuck in the mud. The graded strip was covered with a layer of limestone coarsely broken into three- to six-inch pieces. Over this another layer of limestone, crushed more finely, was spread. Limestone was abundant, not far away, and was both cheaper and better than the occasional gravel deposits. A limestone pike permitted travel at all seasons; heavily loaded wagons did not mire down. After two or three years of use the tracks became fairly smooth except for inevitable "chuck holes" that uneven drainage, freezing, and thawing tended to develop. Maintenance operations were not frequent; regular travelers knew where to expect each bump. A really bad one was called a "thank-you-mom."

Normally the right-of-way was wide enough to permit the piked strip to be laid along one half of the width. The other half, left for use in dry weather, was called the mud or dirt road. Nearly everyone preferred to use the dirt strip when it was dry enough. It was easier on horse, buggy, and passenger. Steel rims did not screech over rough stone, bumps were softer, and hard rubber tires received less wear. In time buggy and wagon wheels wore down two narrow ruts that separated grass-grown strips from the wider center trail trodden smooth by the feet of the buggy horses. During dry summer months the earthen tracks soon became

197

deep in fine dust, pleasant only to the feet of a barefoot boy.

A pike had been built along the south side of our farm a few years before Father and Mother purchased the place. The Kenton pike, as it was known, followed what was reputed once to have been an Indian trail, and angled across the county. Nearly all other roads ran straight east, west, north, or south, a mile apart on section lines. Our house stood on a north and south road about a quarter of a mile north of the Kenton pike. This road was stoned sometime in the late nineties. I can dimly remember the many teams that brought the crushed stone, one cubic yard in a load, in wagons whose beds had bottoms of loose two-by-fours that could be lifted to allow the stone to fall into a pile under the wagons. Men used potato hooks to spread it out. Located as we were, two miles east and two miles south of the nearest corner of Ada, this improvement gave us two all-year routes to town.

The road along the north side of the farm remained unimproved until many years after the motor age arrived. After heavy rains and during the latter part of winter, it became a slippery mire and a great burden to our good neighbors, Will and Eva Powell, who had to use a half-mile of it daily to reach their mail box. Will raised purebred Poland China hogs. The muddy road made hard going when he had to deliver a hog to the express or freight office for shipment.

Whether by pike or dirt road, a wagon journey to Ada and return took a full half-day. Even with the wagon empty for one way, the draft team could not be expected to trot. When wheat was sold, it had to go by wagon to the elevator in town. Now and then hogs had to be hauled to market. More often the wagon brought supplies to the farm—tile, lumber, coal, or fertilizer. For the driver in mild weather this was a leisurely job after his load had been attended to. From his fairly comfortable spring seat he could enjoy the scenery while the horses followed the road. On a cold and windy day he was likely to get down and walk beside the team. One thing he had to watch. If the wagon had stood several days in hot sun in dry weather, the fellies—the wooden arcs supported by the spokes—might shrink enough to loosen the steel tires as the wagon jarred over the hard stones of the pike. If a tire slipped off under a heavy load, as happened with me once, the situation could be embarrassing.

One day I had taken a team and wagon to Ada to bring out an order of drainage tile. The horses moved the heavy load almost without effort over the brick pavement through town. When we reached the pike, they had to pull hard and steadily. Next day, thinking about this striking difference, I mentioned it to Father.

"Wouldn't it be a good thing," I asked, "to pave the main roads through the country just like they do in town?"

"Yes, I think it would," he replied. "But the cost would be prohibitive. A pavement costs several thousand dollars a mile. We farmers are taxed to pay for road improvements along our properties. We would be bankrupted by the expense. It would be nice, but a luxury that farmers couldn't afford."

Neither of us foresaw the multiplication of motor vehicles or the gasoline taxes that have lifted most farm roads out of the mud. Father lived to see the Kenton pike paved. Now it is part of U.S. Route 30S that

199

reaches ocean-to-ocean across the continent from Atlantic City to Astoria, Oregon. The other two roads bordering the farm have long since been blacktopped.

In fair weather travel by buggy was pleasant. One relaxed on the cushioned seat and back, held the reins—we called them "lines"—lightly, and enjoyed every detail of the countryside as the horse jogged along. When one met a neighbor or passed when he was working near the road, custom called for a stop to visit. At night one had the full benefit of moonlight or darkness. Some buggies were equipped with kerosene lights, but ordinarily the lights were considered to be superfluous. A leisurely buggy ride on a comfortable Sunday afternoon or on a warm moonlit night afforded time and opportunity to talk of many things.

Cold and stormy weather, on the other hand, could put downright misery into buggy travel. One wore his thickest and warmest clothing. In wintertime heavy, fleece-lined underwear with long legs and sleeves was standard at all times. For a buggy trip on a cold day an extra pair of trousers was advisable, felt-lined arctic overshoes, a good overcoat, a warm scarf, and a fur or plush cap that covered the ears. If one were stylish or stubborn enough to insist on wearing a hat, he had to put on ear muffs. Thick, warmly lined gloves were a necessity. In such weather the side curtains were always kept on the buggy to break the winds. Once in the buggy the driver and his passenger, if he had one, first tucked a heavy horse blanket and then a fur robe over his legs, under his feet, and secured the edges by sitting on them. Even so, after half an hour the cold began to penetrate and the feet grew icy. For cold drives Mother heated the soapstone to put under our feet. This piece of smooth stone was an inch thick and roughly a foot square. Lifted from the hot stove by a wire handle and wrapped in an old piece of blanket, the soapstone held some of its heat for more than an hour. Some people drove with a lighted kerosene lantern under their laprobes, but Father thought this was dangerous. The buggy carried no magic buttons to turn on heat, light, or music.

If one had to keep to the road during a heavy rainstorm or driving sleet, he spread the rain apron, which fitted over the dashboard and covered the lap. If he got hit in the face he just took it, unless he owned the more elaborate type of rain apron that could be buttoned into the top of the buggy and had an isinglass window to see through and a flap through which to thread the lines. Once at the destination the driver never thought of going inside until he tied the horse and covered him securely with a blanket. In fine weather or bad, the horse-and-buggy traveler had frequent use for a good clothes brush; even if no dust or mud adhered to his clothing, he could depend on finding a few horse hairs.

Most of the neighbors drove plain box buggies like ours. The seat was barely more than wide enough for two adults. A third person could ride but, child or grown-up, had either to sit on someone's lap or squat on a stool between two pairs of legs. For long trips Father used to slip a thin board under the middle of the seat cushion. I rode many a mile astride that projecting board. Phaetons, lower and wider, were owned by a few families and were favored by the more stylish town ladies. Families with numerous children owned two-seated surreys, which, if memory serves, always did have a fringe around the top. The surrey was the station wagon of the Golden Years.

The horse-and-buggy age provided slow transportation at slight cash outlay. The cost of homegrown feed for our $85 Old Doc, while he wore out two $50 buggies and two sets of $20 harness over twenty years, was not much. With respect either to transportation or time, the standard of living was not high compared to the present. Five miles to Ada and back, with time for errands in town, took half a day. Eleven miles to the county seat at Kenton required a full day. For a longer trip one expected to be away over night. The range of travel was limited unless one moved by train.

With his respect for the value of time, Father appreciated the automobile's greater speed. But he was never disposed to risk life or car in the interest of saving time; they were more valuable. The greatest distance he ever drove was probably less than three hundred miles; and it is not likely that his speedometer often registered higher than thirty-five miles an hour. He had no regret that his horse-and-buggy years were a matter of memory. He accepted progress and believed in it.

Chapter 15

The Setting and Some Contrasts

The highest elevation in Ohio stands in the county to the south of our farm, where a Logan County hilltop towers to all of 1,550 feet above sea level. Most of Ohio's rolling beauty lies fifty miles or more to the eastward. Although not quite as level as some of the flat Black Swamp country to our northwest, nearly all the gradients of Hardin County are slight.

Our house stands a mile and a half north of the crest of the Divide, the glacier's terminal moraine, which separates the rain waters. General Robinson's house in Kenton was reputed to stand so exactly on the crest that raindrops falling on the south side of his rooftop traveled by way of the Scioto to the Ohio River, the Mississippi, and the Gulf of Mexico while those from the north roof made their way to Lake Erie, the St. Lawrence, and the Atlantic.

When we drove three miles to McGuffey, which lay just below the crest of the Divide, we were at the edge of the Scioto Marsh. This 17,000-acre tract, for centuries a shallow swamp, had been successfully drained and had become an absolutely level expanse of black, fertile muck. Year after year nearly all of it then was planted in onions. Onion farming was more speculative than ours. In some years midsummer floods drowned the crop, and in others low prices canceled the hopes for profits. Those who survived these calamities kept on trying, because in still other years onions often were extremely profitable.

The muck, all decayed vegetable matter with virtually no mineral content, was quite light in weight. When strong winds blew for long during an extended dry period, the muck rose and went along with the wind. Early spring windstorms could blow out the newly planted onion sets. More than once our window sills, though three and more miles away, were heavily blackened. The muck sometimes caught fire, too, and would burn for days. Between winds and fire over the years the muck tended to disappear and, except where it lay deepest, to become mingled with subsoils. The area still is quite fertile, but not nearly so black, and now grows more corn and soybeans than onions.

A smaller marsh of about 3,000 acres lay four miles north of our farm, and has had much the same history.

The county next north of Hardin was Hancock, and to the west was Allen. In the 1880s both Findlay and Lima, the respective county seats, became famous for the productive oil fields surrounding them. When we traveled north to Wood County, we saw hundreds of flares, wastefully burning the gas from underground for which there was then little or no market. Hopeful wildcatters now and then leased a few acres in Hardin County, including our farm on one occasion, supposing that more oil might be found. Their money and their wells always ran dry.

Our county of Hardin was separated from the Indiana line by two intervening counties, and lay some seventy miles south of Toledo, with Columbus south and east by a slightly shorter distance. Its name came from a man who never traversed its borders. Colonel John Hardin, a Virginia-born officer in the Revolution, was killed by Indians near Sidney in western Ohio in 1792 when he was only thirty-nine years old. At the time he was carrying a message of peace to the Miami tribes.

The county had been formed by the state legislature in 1820, but was not organized until 1833. The county seat was named for the famous Indian fighter, Simon Kenton, then still living. By 1840 the county's population had grown to 4,583; twenty years later it had trebled and by 1880 reached 27,583.

Where did the people come from? The 1880 census breakdown of origins reported that 22,328 had been born in Ohio; 1,047 in Pennsylvania; 480 in Virginia; 320 in New York; 187 in Indiana; 85 in Kentucky; 738 in the German empire; 386 in Ireland; 147 in England or Wales; 57 in British America; 20 in Scotland; and 18 in France.

The first railroad train to enter the county reached Kenton on July 4, 1846. It brought a load of excursionists from Sandusky, on Lake Erie. The road was called the Mad River and Lake Erie, and ran from Sandusky to Dayton.

In 1852 another railroad crossed the county through the northern tier of townships. It was to become the main line of what is now the Penn Central's New York to Chicago route. A little later the Erie ran its tracks east and west through the center of the county, and the Toledo and Ohio Central came north and south, connecting Toledo with Columbus and West Virginia's coal fields.

The hamlet of Huntersville, a mile east of the farm, had its beginnings in 1839. A long-forgotten Thomas Hitchcock had "laid out" town lots and for reasons apparently unrecorded named his settlement Huntersville in honor of an equally long-forgotten Jabez Hunter. During its first decade Huntersville had boasted a general store and post office. I have often wondered whether anywhere a single "Huntersville, Ohio" postmark survives. The railroads to its north and south left Huntersville to become merely a wide place at a bend of the Kenton pike, where the church, the blacksmith shop, and later only the Grange hall and a half-dozen houses were to remain.

Ada, our trading center, had been established in the 1850s, and a half-century later had become a pleasant village of slightly more than 2,000 inhabitants. Though it was twice as far from the farm as McGuffey, Father probably preferred Ada because it offered good banking service and better stores. As the site of Ohio Northern University, Ada in many respects was and is a better-than-average town of its size. The present population stands at about 5,000.

By the time Father and Mother bought their farm in 1891, few vestiges of Hardin County's original condition remained. Once all the area except the marshes had been heavily forested. The cultivated land had been cleared in the early years; few of the fields being plowed had so much as a single stump left. To the south of our house one shapely maple had been left standing in the middle of the best field. A half-day's work would have converted it into firewood. Year after year Father farmed around it. He left it stand merely because it was a beautiful tree and he liked to look at it.

Woodlots of ten or twenty acres or larger remained on most farms. They yielded fuel for the stoves that heated the houses and held the kitchen fires. Occasional logs and fence posts could be cut. Here and there a great old tree from the virgin stand might remain, but they were few. The scattered woodlots were numerous enough that from almost any point in the area one would see trees between himself and the horizon.

When the forests were cleared, thousands of logs had been split into rails to make the first fences. Rails were durable. Enough of them remained on our place to serve for at least a half-mile of Father's first fences. He knew how to build the rails into an efficient barrier, "horse high, bull strong and hog tight," whether in zigzag design or the stake and rider type. As the old rails rotted and gave way, they were consigned to the wood-pile, and eventually all the fences were of tight-strung woven wire. If properly built of heavy, well-galvanized wire, these fences, too, were durable, and had the advantage that they occupied less ground space than the rails did. The end posts and corner posts had to be correctly set and well braced. When every field was enclosed every bit of growth, including weeds, could be pastured by sheep and converted into salable flesh and wool.

Except for our weather-boarded old house, almost none of the log structures put up by original settlers had survived into the 1890s. After the Civil War they had been superseded by frame structures, mostly simple in design, unornamented, but sturdily built; many are still standing and still in use. A few of the farmhouses were built of brick on plain and unpretentious lines. There were no mansions.

Farms ranged widely in size. A few people owned as much as 300 acres. Many made their livings on eighty acres, and some who owned no more than forty acres appeared to live comfortably. Our 125 acres was about average.

Father was not "land hungry." Had he been ambitious to expand his acreage, he would have found it difficult to do in the immediate neighborhood. When farms changed hands at all, it was usually only when an owner died and had no heirs willing or able to take over. On his 125 acres Father managed to keep himself, a hired man, and in summer two teams busy at profitable work. Horse power was a limiting factor in considering expansion. Additional land, unless for pasturage, would have meant keeping more horses as well as hiring more help. He thought that our place was about the right size for economical operation. Besides, he was not competitive. Whether he was first to plant corn or whether his wheat outyielded the neighbors' did not concern him. The guiding intent was to run a profitable farm.

To farm today in most parts of the Midwest with the standards of efficiency Father would demand, the requirements are different. A mere 125 acres would not do. At least 350 to 400 acres—or even a full 640-acre section or more, depending upon crop and animal programs followed—would be needed. Although the labor would cost much more, the actual amount of it would be little greater, and probably less. The investment in power and machinery would be immensely greater— from $75,000 up. The cash outlay for fertilizer would be far higher. Cash for weedicides and insecticides, wholly unknown then, would require substantial sums.

For the wheat harvest Father used the grain binder, for which he paid $120. Two hands shocked the wheat. Then the hired threshing machine came, along with a dozen or so neighbors with their teams, whom we in turn helped when they threshed. The same work on a 400-acre farm today, with three times as much wheat to harvest, is performed by one or two men in much less time. But the combine-harvester to do the job may cost $15,000.

Father's investment in horse power, for two teams, was no more than $500; their hay and grain grew on the farm. They required no gasoline or oil, and needed no expensive repairs. The tractor for today's efficient 400-acre farm could cost $8,000. The owner also will usually have in use an older or smaller one.

Those who know only the cash economy of today's agriculture may not easily understand why those 1900–1915 years could have been regarded as "golden." During the latter part of the period Father was selling hogs at from $4.10 to $7.00 per hundredweight; oats at 50 cents a bushel, wheat at 86 cents and corn at 75 cents. Wool brought 20 to 23 cents a pound, lambs $6.50, and sheep $3.25.

Part of the answer may be seen when the other side of his ledger notes that a hair cut and shave cost him 30 cents, shoes $4, hat $3, suit of clothes $17.90, and sugar was five cents a pound. His tailor-made suit cost $26.50, and lasted him for years.

The fields were fertilized almost wholly by the manure produced by animals fed on the place, along with the straw and cornstalks that provided their bedding. Not until 1912 did the first order for a commercial fertilizer, 2,500 pounds of acid phosphate, come to show what it could add to the farm's output.

Living expenses, too, were modest. All the vegetables, practically all the meat, all the butter, milk, and eggs, and some of the fruit we ate were homegrown. Even though the income figures were small, the outgo was always smaller.

The bigger acreages, the bigger machinery, and the necessary power equipment of these days were not among Father's problems. His last decade saw the early efforts to adapt tractor power to smaller farms such as ours, and to adapt the horse-drawn machinery to the faster and more powerful tractor. He observed the experiences of the one or two neighbors who were converting to the tractor regime. Not until three or four years after his passing did horses finally leave the farm. Then, while I was trying to manage by long distance, we acquired a new renter who used tractor power. This was early in the 1930s, when prices for farm products fell lower than they had been ten years earlier. Walter Schantz, the new renter, was a skilled hog breeder. His semi-annual auction sales of purebred Hampshires brought prices well above those paid for market hogs. Before 1940 he had saved enough money to buy a farm of his own. It seemed that Father's memory might be better honored by putting the farm in Walter's capable hands than by trying, from 700 miles away, to operate with the uncertainties of a new partner. So, now for more than a third of a century, the L. D. McMillen farm has been the Schantz farm.

Chapter 16

The Later Years

For thirty-eight years Father saw the springs come to enliven his 125-acre domain, watched the new seeds sprout and grow, and each autumn looked upon the harvest. Through nearly four changing decades he attended the crops, fought the weeds, gave kind and vigilant care to the animals, and kept abreast of new and better ideas as they appeared.

He had observed his thirty-third birthday on May 8, 1891, by planting corn for the first time in fields that he could call his own. His threescore and ten mark came in 1928. In November of that year, after the harvests were in, the one serious illness of his career ended his time on earth.

After the 1900–1915 "golden years" the stability of that era faded out. Both costs and prices rose. They rose unevenly, and farmers found it harder to anticipate what management courses should be pursued. In general, however, Father followed the programs he had previously found profitable, and in most years found this plan better than trying to accommodate to the rapidly shifting situations. As usual, in one way or another, he met the challenges of change and the fluctuations of prices and weather.

As always, he was resourceful. The summer of 1915 brought an unusually good wheat crop, and wheat was in demand. Unseasonable rains, climaxed by a June flood, had left the nineteen-acre wheatfield so soggy and muddy that part of it could not possibly be harvested by the binder. The straw had lodged, and the prospect for saving the down grain looked dim. From some source Father obtained two old-time cradles, such as he had known how to use before the binder became common. The cradle, for the benefit of anyone who may not know, was in principle a scythe to which, above and curved parallel with the blade, a number of wooden fingers were attached. These collected the straw and, as the harvester reversed his swing, left the grain in neat windrows ready to be bound into bundles. He not only located the cradles, but found that our good neighbor, Stimp Bloodworth, remembered how they should be used. The two of them swung the antiquated implements across the three or four acres of sodden ground and thereby saved a hundred or more bushels of good wheat.

The new arrangement, with a renter providing the labor, taking a share of the responsibility, and receiving a third of the income, provided Father with more opportunity to relax. He continued to make the business decisions—always after talking them out with the tenant—and contributed far more actual labor to these partnerships than the agreements demanded. As the owner it was his job to maintain the plant, to look after fences, buildings, repairs and such details. But he couldn't stop at that. If a man needed another hand to drive a team or operate a pitchfork, he could not stand by. The working habits of too many decades remained in control.

He did make one change. During most winters from 1914 on he and Mother took off for a few weeks in Florida. In Bradenton they made dozens of new friends among townspeople and their fellow tourists, enjoyed the mild weather and the various kinds of entertainment. By March 1 they were sure to be home again. Father could not bear to see a new farm year begin without being on hand to take part in it.

In 1918 he acquired a new partner. In January he wrote that he and Mother had decided to rent the farm on another basis, and that they would move to Ada.

I was in the process of selling the Indiana weekly newspaper, which had been an instructive but not financially profitable experience. I had no definite plans, and the farm appealed to me as it never had done in earlier days. "Don't rent until I see you," I wired, and hurried to Ohio. By early March the paper was sold, and I was back between the plow handles, delighted to be free from soliciting advertising, wrestling with balky printing machinery, and worrying about forthcoming bills.

For four and a half years, through five crop seasons, we worked happily in partnership, fifty-fifty. That is, I assumed ownership of the working equipment and furnished the labor; he provided the land and capital maintenance. The proceeds we split equally. I had some new ideas that he questioned; but we talked them out, and he did all he could to make them succeed. I believed that raising hogs at that period would pay better than feeding cattle. He liked handling cattle better, but went along cheerfully with the plans for building a swine herd. Although we ran into the beginnings of the agricultural depression that struck in late 1920, we managed to make some money each year.

Unexpected and out of the blue one day came the offer of a job in New York as an editor of *Farm and Fireside,* then one of the leading national farm magazines. The salary was generous enough, even for living in New York. I was hesitant. We were having a good time together on the farm and getting ahead.

"It's for your good, son. You had better go," he said. He pointed out that the farm would always demand a certain amount of hard, physical labor, and that there could come (as there did) another era of difficult times. "If this job doesn't work out for you," he added, "the farm will always be here." He made prompt arrangements to finish out the year's tasks and to find a new renter. Later on, when I suggested that I wanted to repay the money he had advanced during the newspaper episode, he bluntly refused. "That," he wrote, "I have always considered to be a part of your education. Of course we hoped that it would have turned out better financially. But after all I think it was a good investment for both of us, and I know you have made good use of the experience."

He closed the letter with another remark that reflected his appreciation for other than monetary considerations. "The girl you got there is a fortune to you and to the rest of us."

No judgment he ever uttered could have been more correct. "The girl" and I had nearly fifty-nine fortunate and happy years together. Although she could not live to see it here, I rejoice that she had seen

214

Father's statement in the manuscript and knew that it was to be in the book.

About his financial status Father was never communicative. Whether he made or lost money on a livestock feeding winter he made no mention. If he talked to Mother about such matters, she was the only human being in whom he confided. His bankers, of course, had a pretty good idea of his standing at most times, although they probably knew little more than could be read from his deposits and withdrawals. The banking custom of requiring detailed financial statements from customers was not then thoroughly established.

One day toward the close of his life, when we were talking about years that had gone by, he said, "I have always thought I ought to be able to save at least a thousand dollars a year. Most years I have done it, but not always."

Until after the "golden years" period he kept a meticulous account of income and disbursements. Those records he left behind him. They are inconclusive as to his net gains. They mention loans of sums from $100 to $2,000 to his brothers, to neighbors, and to others, but do not record the repayments in such manner that anyone but an accountant, and perhaps not even one skilled in such matters, could tell exactly how he came out on each transaction. Whether all these were repaid or not, he did not indicate. Most of them certainly were, especially such as the considerable amounts he lent to the school board in anticipation of tax collections.

With two or three exceptions, his few non-farm investments apparently turned out well. After a June fortnight in Colorado in 1903, probably to please a friend, he put $250 in a gold mining enterprise which turned out to be worthless. He invested $1,000 and became a director of an Ada company formed to manufacture the fire alarm system devised by a local inventor. The system worked, but was hard to sell, and the company eventually failed. His telephone company stock, bank stock, and occasional investments in local bonds and mortgages paid their dividends or interest and some appreciated in value.

The farm itself, however, he felt was always his best investment. He could figure when an improvement or a livestock purchase was likely to pay off.

Toward the close of the war years a visitor from a nearby county, one of the friends he had made in Florida, offered $200 an acre for the farm which, in 1891, had been purchased for $35. He declined the offer. "I don't know how to invest the money to better advantage," he said, "and I wouldn't know what to do with myself without the farm."

When he wrote in the late twenties about his recent purchase of a new automobile, he said that "it seems like a piece of extravagance, but we will enjoy it. I have always managed to live within our income. Economy has always stood out in big letters before me, and no doubt always will."

One March day while we were in partnership, he had come out from town as usual in the morning to help with whatever project we had under way. While we were at the noonday table, a violent blizzard started. I took advantage of the inclemency to do a little desk work. When I went to find him in midafternoon, I heard a tinkle of iron from the workshop. He was standing at the bench straightening rusty nails so they could be used again.

I laughed at him. "Not making very big wages, are you?"

With hammer dangling in one hand and a bent nail still in the other, he faced me with his reply. "I have always thought that when I worked I would like to make a dollar an hour; but I would rather make a nickel an hour than not to make anything."

Neither waste nor extravagance of time or substance found any place in his way of life. He practiced economy without a trace of miserliness. He was genuinely industrious. But these qualities were not unique. It was being the studious manager who combined boldness with caution, who made informed judgments and acted by his convictions, that won his success.

"Your father never offered anyone advice," one of the neighborhood's most propserous younger farmers once told me. "Many times when I had a business problem, I went to talk to him about it. He never told me what to do, but somehow by the time I left I had made up my mind, and the decision would turn out to be right. I owe him a lot."

While he lay in a hospital bed during the first attack of his terminal illness, Father made plain what had been a major goal in his thoughts. I had left the room for an hour or so to attend to errands.

"A nurse came in while you were out and I was dozing," he said when he awakened after I returned. "She left something over there on the dresser. What was it?" I told him it was the bill for his first week in the hospital, that I had found it and had taken it down to the office and paid it.

"Get me my checkbook!" he demanded. "Your mother and I have worked and saved all these years so that we could always take care of ourselves and never be dependent on anyone. Not even on you! You are not going to pay our bills."

Independence! That was it. He had always wanted to be a free American, living on and within his own resources, unobligated to anyone for favors or support, able to chart his own course and to make his own decisions. One reason he liked the farm was that it was a business he could run without becoming obligated to others or having to kowtow to anyone.

He was a success. He had so managed his 125 acres and his way of living that his purpose was accomplished.

During the ten years that Mother survived him, she was able to spend winters with her Florida friends, and at no time wanted for comfort or care. She and Father had not been rich in money or goods, as riches are measured, but they lived in what they considered plenty; and when she was gone, a few thousands were left over.

It would not be fitting to close this volume without alluding again to a remark on one of the opening pages. Father would have called himself an average farmer, and I said there that he was above average, not typical perhaps, but in the best sense, representative. Across the country, not only in the Midwest, whose ways I have tried to describe, but from coast to coast in those years tens of thousands of farmers were much like him. They prized independence; they were hardworking, honorable, economical, and generally public-spirited citizens. Nor were they peculiar to those "golden years"; tens of thousands of farmers are like that now as they cultivate their broader acres with machines and techniques then unknown. Those of the past and those of the present, I salute them all.

After his death, *Farm and Fireside* printed a piece I wrote about him. The article told something of his farming career and of the personal principles by which he lived. The first few paragraphs were the important ones; and they, perhaps, will reveal why I have so earnestly wanted to produce this book. Here they are:

"While his neighbors stood bareheaded in the November sunshine, while brown and yellow leaves rattled along the gravel paths, Mother and I watched the return to earth of Father's mortal form. The soil, in which he had labored for more than half a century, is his resting place. He is at the end of the furrow.

"He had passed his threescore and ten. The loss of one's father is inevitable, perhaps therefore a little more endurable. But Dad was the friend to whom I went, in trouble or in triumph, with complete certainty of understanding. He lifted me over hard places. He rejoiced when I made them alone.

"We were more than father and son, Dad and I. We were friends, very personal friends.

"Here on my desk is the notification that there has come to me an honor for which I have long secretly hoped; nothing great, but a gratifying milestone. Yet, somehow, it might as well not have come. For I can't tell Dad about it. Before this, an interesting experience was twice pleasurable—when it happened, and when I shared it with him.

"As my closest friend he was proud and pleased with every bit of good fortune that came to me. But no more than I was proud of him!"

Corn Cob syrup- P. 60